The
First Gospel

The Aramaic Gospel Before
Matthew, Mark, Luke, and John

Robert E. Aldridge

WestBow
P R E S S
A DIVISION OF THOMAS NELSON

WestBow Press books may be ordered through booksellers or by contacting:

WestBow Press
A Division of Thomas Nelson
1663 Liberty Drive
Bloomington, IN 47403
www.westbowpress.com
1-(866) 928-1240

Because of the dynamic nature of the Internet, any web addresses or links contained in this book may have changed since publication and may no longer be valid. The views expressed in this work are solely those of the author and do not necessarily reflect the views of the publisher, and the publisher hereby disclaims any responsibility for them.

Any people depicted in stock imagery provided by Thinkstock are models, and such images are being used for illustrative purposes only.

Certain stock imagery © Thinkstock.

ISBN: 978-1-4497-1428-4 (sc)
ISBN: 978-1-4497-1430-7 (hc)
ISBN: 978-1-4497-1429-1 (e)

Library of Congress Control Number: 2011925481

Printed in the United States of America

WestBow Press rev. date: 5/20/2011

*To my sister Anna, for her love
and support throughout the years*

Table of Contents

Preface

In the early 1990s I began an in-depth study of early Christian beliefs, history, and literature, with heavy use of primary sources. The present work is one of many products of that study and has been written for several reasons.

First, since it was inevitable that evidence of Matthew's real gospel as the major literary source of the synoptic gospels would one day be made public, to do so in a manner that defends historic Christianity, rather than to have this information twisted by anti-Christian writers into "proof" that the New Testament gospels were later distortions and falsifications of the original eyewitness account.

Second, to destroy (hopefully) the theory of Q, a pernicious and untrue theory which is being used to attack the Christian faith. This theory claims that a lost document, alleged to be the basis for two of the gospels, derived from ancient wisdom collections and from a community that did not view Jesus as the Savior, Messiah, and Son of God.

And third, to provide evangelists and those defending Christianity with a better understanding of the origin of the gospels and additional arguments for their truth and historicity.

The present work is a pioneering study and I hope that other works follow that will expand and refine the evidence on this subject. Gloria Deo!

North Hollywood, California
December 2010

About the Apostle Matthew

Jesus had twelve disciples: "The first, Simon, who is called Peter, and Andrew his brother; James the son of Zebedee, and John his brother; Philip, and Bartholomew; Thomas, and Matthew the publican; James the son of Alphaeus, and Lebbeus, whose surname was Thaddeus; Simon the Cananaean, and Judas Iscariot, who also betrayed him" (Matt 10:2-4). Matthew's name in Hebrew was *Mattiyah*, meaning "the gift of Yah."

Jesus called Matthew to be His disciple in this manner: "And as Jesus passed forth from thence, He saw a man, named Matthew, sitting at the receipt of custom: and He saith unto him, *Follow Me*. And he arose, and followed Him" (Matt 9:9). This happened at Capernaum, where Jesus then lived. In the Gospel of Mark's version of this event, and in Luke 5: 27, Matthew is called Levi: "And as He passed by, He saw Levi the son of Alphaeus sitting at the receipt of custom, and said unto him, *Follow Me*. And he arose and followed Him" (Mk 2:14).

The tax-collector Matthew, who must have kept extensive records of taxes paid and owed, was probably the only one of the Twelve who knew how to read and write. This picture of Matthew from a medieval manuscript of about 820 AD (re-drawn by the author) shows him writing his gospel at a scribe's work-station.

Matthew had been a tax-collector. As a tax-collector, he kept detailed records of the taxes each family had paid, of what they still owed, and possibly of what each family owned. Tax-collectors were hated by the Jews because they were agents of Rome. Judea had been subject to Rome since

63 BC, and Roman troops occupied the country from 6 AD on, treating the Jewish people very roughly. The Jews were forced to pay taxes to finance their own occupation.

Tax-collectors were also hated because they were often corrupt, taking more money than they should in order to make themselves rich. They were seen as traitors who sold their services to the Roman oppressors, and used inquisitorial methods to make money at the expense of their fellow countrymen. The phrase "tax-collectors and sinners" occurs many times in the New Testament. The rabbinical writings call them robbers. Tax-collectors were traitors, sinners, and social outcasts.

Yet Jesus called Matthew the tax-collector to be one of His disciples. Jesus' association with tax-collectors and sinners was scandalous to the Pharisees and other self-righteous people. He did this because He came to call sinners to repentance, and Matthew was a clear example of a forgiven sinner. Matthew was joyful for his deliverance, and held a dinner for Jesus at his house, at which he introduced Jesus to his tax-collector friends. Matthew may have been the disciple who was most grateful to Jesus, and in time he found a way to try to repay his gratitude. For he was the only one of the Twelve who could read and write.[1]

---

1   The present writer believes that John's writings were written through a personal secretary or scribe.

CHAPTER 1

The Sayings of Our Lord

1. *The Testimony of Eusebius and Papias*

About 325 AD Eusebius Pamphili, Bishop of Caesarea, completed his famous *Church History*, which told the story of the Church up until the time of Emperor Constantine. Book Three of his work discusses the martyrs and literature of the Apostolic Church. Chapter 24 tells how the gospels were written, and speaks first of Matthew. After the Crucifixion, the Apostle Matthew spent twelve years preaching in Jerusalem[2] before undertaking his missionary journey to Persia, where he was martyred.[3] Chapter 24 says that "Matthew, who had at first preached to the Hebrews, when he was about to go to other peoples, committed his gospel to writing in his native tongue, and thus compensated those whom he was obliged to leave for the loss of his presence." Eusebius then goes on to discuss the other gospels. By beginning with Matthew, however, he implies that Matthew's gospel was written first, before the apostle's journey to Persia about 40 AD.[4] This is not the Gospel of Matthew found in the New Testament, but another work.

Chapter 39 of the same book discusses the writings of Papias, Bishop of Hierapolis (in what is now central Turkey) in the early second century.

---

2   It was a tradition of the early Church that for twelve years after the Crucifixion all the Apostles remained in Jerusalem ministering to their fellow Jews (Eusebius, *Church History,* 5.18, and Clement of Alexandria, *Miscellanies,* 6.5). However, there was also another tradition that Matthew spent fifteen years preaching in Jerusalem before his departure.

3   According to another tradition, Matthew was martyred in Ethiopia south of the Caspian Sea (in eastern Pontus, not Africa).

4   According to Eusebius's *Church History* (5.8.2), Irenaeus stated that "Matthew published among the Hebrews a writing of the gospel in their own language, while Peter and Paul were in Rome preaching the gospel and founding the Church." It is unclear whether Irenaeus meant that Matthew produced his gospel specifically between the years 50?-62/64 AD, or more generally in the period between the Crucifixion and the creation of Mark's gospel, and using the founding of the Church at Rome as a dramatic event representative of that period.

Papias was well-informed about the first-century Church. He was a friend of Polycarp (St. John's disciple), and knew Philip the Evangelist (one of the seven deacons mentioned in Acts 6:5), who also lived in Hierapolis. About 130 AD Papias wrote a book, *The Interpretation of the Dominical Sayings,* which presumably explained Jesus' more difficult sayings. Although *The Interpretation* has not survived, Eusebius gives several excerpts from it in his *Church History,* including a statement on the first gospel of Matthew, called *The Sayings of Our Lord:* "Matthew composed *The Sayings* in the Hebrew language, and each interpreted [or translated] them as best as he could."

Eusebius's *Church History*

In 231 AD, Origen, the most famous theologian of the early Church, moved from Alexandria to Caesarea (in northern Palestine) and established a large library there, which focused on Bible texts. Origen died in 255 AD. About 280 AD Pamphilus, then bishop of Caesarea, founded a school and expanded Origen's library. Pamphilus' library contained a large number of early Christian writings, including important second-century works such as Papias' *Interpretation of the Dominical Sayings* (c. 130 AD), Hegesippus' *Memoirs* (c. 180 AD), Clement of Alexandria's *Outlines* (c. 190 AD), and many others -- all now lost.

Eusebius was a native of Caesarea and a pupil of Pamphilus who helped him organize and edit Origen's Bible collection. In the 290s Eusebius used Pamphilus' library to write most of his *Church History* (the last three chapters were written in 324-25 AD). The library's large collection of rare books, often by eyewitness to the events they narrated, enabled Eusebius to create an invaluable account of the Church's early history. Most of the works that Eusebius cites are now lost and Eusebius' quotations are all that remain of them. Pamphilus was martyred about 315 AD and Eusebius succeeded him as bishop of Caesarea.

---

2. Several Observations

Let us make several observations. First, regarding when *The Sayings* was written. Since Jesus was born about 6 BC -- Herod the Great, who died in 4 BC, had ordered the killing of all children in the neighborhood of Bethlehem who were two years old or younger -- and was about 30 years old when He began His ministry (Luke 3:23), His ministry must have begun about 24 AD, or possibly a year or two later. And since Pilate became governor of Judea in 25 AD and the fact that it was his custom to pardon a condemned prisoner at Passover implies he had done it several times before, the Crucifixion may have occurred about 28 AD. Therefore "twelve years after the Crucifixion" means *The Sayings* was given to the Jerusalem Church about 40 AD. It was the first Christian writing, predating the Apostolic Decree (about 48 AD) and Paul's first epistle, 1 Thessalonians (about 50 AD).[5]

```
+-----------------------------------------------+
|         Chronology of The Sayings             |
|                                               |
|    6 BC -- Birth of Jesus                     |
|   28 AD -- The Crucifixion                    |
|   40 AD -- The Sayings is written             |
|   65 AD -- Gospel of Mark is written          |
|   70 AD -- Gospel of Luke is written          |
|   75 AD -- Gospel of Matthew is written       |
+-----------------------------------------------+
```

Second, it is unlikely that the work Matthew gave to the Church about 40 AD was composed from scratch at that time. It was probably a presentation copy of a writing he had been working on for a long time. His sources were his own memory and the memories of other apostles and followers. (The role of the Holy Spirit will be considered further on.) It may have begun as a collection of sayings (*logia*), to which parables, dialogues, and short incidents were later added -- which were afterwards arranged into a narrative. It must have gone through several versions over the years. And there are good reasons for believing that the narrative section was later placed in front of the earlier *logia* material -- perhaps when it was being prepared for presentation to the Church. The final edition was a stripped-down version of the Gospel of Matthew found in the New Testament, generally but not exactly in the same order.

Third, Eusebius makes the statement that "when Matthew was about to go to other peoples, he committed his Gospel to writing... and thus compensated those whom he was obliged to leave for the loss of his presence." This implies that Matthew functioned as the keeper of Jesus' sayings (and doings) for the Jerusalem Church. He was a major part of the Church's living memory of Jesus. This underscores the probability that Matthew had been writing down Jesus' sayings and doings for a long time.

Fourth, "Hebrew" means Aramaic, which was then the popular speech

---

5   Some scholars believe that Galatians was written before 1 Thessalonians.

of Palestine.[6] Jesus and the Apostles spoke Aramaic -- and only Aramaic. Jesus' actual Aramaic words are preserved in several places in the New Testament. Eusebius says that "Matthew composed his gospel in his native tongue," which was Palestinian Aramaic.[7] (See Appendix A.)

Fifth, according to Papias, the Apostle Matthew called his gospel Λόγια τοῦ ἡμῶν Κυρίου, which translates into English as *The Sayings of Our Lord*. The original Aramaic must have been זרמד אלמ, which transliterates as *Melê de-Māran*. (See Appendix B.)

Sixth, since the note-book layout of the codex was particularly useful for a tax-collector (and Matthew surely had extras at home), it is likely that *The Sayings* was written as a codex. This is another reason, besides ease of reference, why the early Church adopted the codex for its literature. (It is quite difficult to look for a Scripture passage in a scroll, which cannot be flipped through, but must be unrolled column by column from one end, alternating with slowly rolling up the examined columns toward the other end.) When the canonical gospels were written later, they may have imitated the codex format of the first gospel. (See Appendix C.)

Seventh, Eusebius's statement that "each interpreted them as best as he could" probably means that there were many amateur renderings of *The Sayings* into Greek. One of these anonymous translations may have provided the basic Greek text from which the canonical Gospel of Matthew was created.

Eighth, before the composition of the canonical Gospels later in the first century, *The Sayings* was commonly referred to as "the Gospel" or "the Gospel of our Lord," both evidenced by the *Didache* (written about 60 AD).

And ninth, about 405 AD Jerome wrote his *Commentary on the Gospel of Matthew*. In chapter 12 he writes "In the Gospel which is used by the Nazoreans and the Ebionites.... and which is called by many the real Gospel of Matthew..." (*In Evangelio, quo utuntur Nazaraeni et Ebionitae... et quod vocatur a plerisque Matthaei authenticum*). The early Church didn't completely forget Matthew's Hebrew gospel, and its place as the First Gospel.

---

6   Partial confirmation that *The Sayings* was written in Aramaic is given by Jerome (about 415 AD) who refers to "the Gospel according to the Hebrews, which is actually in the Chaldean and Syrian language but is written in Hebrew letters, and which the Nazoreans use to this day..." (*Adv. Pelag.* 3.2, given in Migne, PL 23, col. 570). *The Gospel according to the Hebrews* was one of several names by which *The Sayings* was later known. However, the Nazoreans didn't use use the original *Sayings of Our Lord,* but a later version that had been modified to reflect their beliefs (to be discussed below).

7   Much has been written on the Aramaic substratum of much of the New Testament. I will only cite Matthew Black, *An Aramaic Approach to the Gospels and Acts* (3rd ed., 1967).

Sayings Gospels

A sayings gospel, in its purest form, is a collection of unrelated or only loosely related sayings, of varying lengths, with no narrative framework, and usually in no particular order.

Several sayings gospels survive from antiquity, including the *Gospel of Thomas,* the *Dialogue of the Savior,* the *Apocryphon of James,* and the *Gospel of Mary,* all of which are Gnostic writings. *Thomas* is a sayings gospel of the purest form, while the others have loose dialogue or thematic structures.

The canonical gospels have narrative formats because they are structured to present the life of Jesus. Many Gnostic writings, on the other hand, are structured as sayings gospels (informal collections of sayings) because they are intended to present Gnostic ideas.

(See Appendix E, item 10 regarding the *Gospel of Thomas.*)

CHAPTER 2

The Didache

This chapter is devoted to the *Didache*[8] because the *Didache* is an important witness to *The Sayings*. The *Didache* (whose common title in antiquity translates as *The Teaching of the Apostles*) is a first-century church-manual that was discovered in 1873 after having been lost for a thousand years. It is a very important document for understanding the early Church. It's about 2,200 words in Greek (3,000 in English), about the length of Galatians or a slightly-long *Reader's Digest* article. The *Didache* is a composite work, with several parts from different sources that were assembled into a single work about 60 AD. Modern scholars have divided it into 16 sections.

1. The Didache's several parts

Sections 1-5 give the text of the *Two Ways*, a Jewish moral treatise that may have been created in the first century BC, possibly for use by God-fearers that attended synagogue. The *Two Ways* begins with a long list of do's and dont's (especially targeting pagan practices), then describes how believers are to behave toward one another. These things are the "Way of Life." The last segment of the *Two Ways* lists many types of evil behavior, the "Way of Death." In the "Way of Life", verses 4:9-11 contain a household code that may have served as the model for Paul's household codes (Col 3:18-4.1 and Eph 5:21-6:9) and likely inspired the household code in 1 Peter 2:18-3:7.

---

8   The word *didache*, meaning *teaching*, has four acceptable pronunciations. The standard pronunciation is like the middle syllables in the sentence "he did a k-turn."

The *Didache*'s several parts, which were joined together about 60 AD

TWO WAYS Chap. 1-5	CHURCH MANUAL Chap. 6-15	FINALE Chap. 16
50 BC?	about 60 AD	date uncertain

The *Two Ways*' opening lines are "there are two ways, one of life and one of death, and there is a great difference between the two ways." A variation of this appears in the Sermon on the Mount: "Enter ye in at the [constricted] gate; for wide is the gate and broad is the way that leadeth to destruction, and many there be which go in thereat. Because [constricted] is the gate and narrow is the way which leadeth unto life. And few there be that find it" (Matt. 7:13-14). The Apostle Peter often used the *Two Ways* as a base-text for his sermons, and the early Church considered him to have written the *Two Ways* at least until the eighth century.[9] The *Two Ways* was used as a catechism of Christian behavior for new believers, until catechisms of belief (like those used today) were created in the fourth century.

Sections 6-15 constitute the church-manual proper. Section 6 touches on the Jewish food laws in a manner similar to Paul ("bear what you can"). Section 7 discusses baptizing new believers. Section 8 speaks about fasting and gives the Lord's Prayer. Sections 9 and 10 give instructions for the Eucharist. Sections 11-12 discuss how to handle itinerant prophets and how to receive those who want to join a Christian community. Both sections include rules for determining phonies. Section 13 concerns giving first-fruits to the prophets ("for they are your high-priests") or directly to the poor. Section 14 concerns breaking bread on the Lord's Day. Section 15 concerns appointing bishops and deacons. And section 16 speaks of Christ's return.

2. The Didache's unusual features

The church-manual contains some materials that appear to come from earlier sources. The *Two Ways* (sections 1-5) was a pre-existing Jewish moral treatise. The liturgy in sections 9-10 was surely already in use, but local eucharists no doubt varied widely. Sections 11-12, on handling itinerant prophets and converts that don't want to work, are not in the church-manual's usually concise style and may have been drawn from another source. (It is even

---

9   See my article "Peter and the Two Ways" in *Vigiliae Christianae,* August 1999.

possible that questions to the Jerusalem authorities about these sensitive issues may have prompted the *Didache's* creation, and that sections 11-12 were the core around which the rest of the *Didache* was constructed.) And there are reasons for believing that section 16 also came from elsewhere.

Scholars have long been puzzled by the absence of certain key Christian elements from the *Didache*. First, the *Didache's* eucharist has a very different significance than that of the traditional Christian eucharist. The eucharistic bread and wine don't represent Jesus' body and blood. Instead the wine represents "the holy vine of... David which [God] has made known to us through [His] servant Jesus." The grape-vine is the traditional symbol of Judaism, and here it refers to one of the promises of Judaism, resurrection, spoken of in Psalm 16, written by David. Verses 8-11 are quoted in Acts 2:25-28 as proof of resurrection.

The bread represents the Church "scattered upon the mountains" that will "be gathered together from the ends of the earth into [God's] kingdom." "Scattered upon the mountains" is an Old Testament phrase referring to Jewish exile outside the land of Israel, and refers here to Christian Jews living in the diaspora. "Gathered... from the ends of the earth" connects with Matt 24:31 ("and He shall send His angels... and they shall gather together His elect from the four winds, from one end of heaven to the other"). All this is very different from the eucharist of the canonical gospels, which is absent from the *Didache*.

In addition, *presbyteroi* (priests or elders, who are often mentioned in Paul's writings) are not mentioned anywhere in the *Didache*, even in the instructions for the eucharist. (Although Jewish high-priests are mentioned in section 13.) Although Jesus' resurrection is clearly stated, there is no reference anywhere to His death as an atonement for sin. (This is the <u>core</u> of Pauline Christianity.) Jesus is never referred to as "the Son of God" or by any title that would imply divinity. Instead, He is called "the Lord" (8:2 and 9:5) and "the servant (*pahis*) of God" (9:2-3 and 10:2). There is no reference to Jesus' virgin birth. It is to be expected that some of these things might not appear in a short description of early Christian belief and practice. But the absence of <u>all of them</u> is telling.

3. The Didache's origin

All of the absent elements were matters of disagreement between Paul's followers and many of the Jewish Christians (primarily the tradition-keeping Jewish Christians who comprised a large part of the Jerusalem

Church).[10] In addition, the *Didache*'s full title is *The Teaching of the Lord to the Gentiles by the Twelve Apostles*, and it contains material connected with the apostles Peter and Matthew (discussed in the following section), and possibly material connected with other apostles that is not recognized as such today. Based on this, a reasonable explanation of the *Didache*'s origin is that it was issued with high authority in the Jewish church about 60 AD. Its purpose was primarily to establish common practices between Jewish and Gentile Christians, without giving offense to either side, in order to foster unity in a Church that was drifting apart; and secondarily to combat the imposters and financial con-men that were preying on Christian communities at that time (which was easy to do because the early Church was deeply committed to sharing).[11]

The *Didache* was issued on high authority, probably from the Jerusalem Church, invoked the Twelve Apostles, and was likely authorized by James the Just or Jude. It cannot have been produced after 70 AD, when the successor Church at Pella was no longer regarded by Gentile Christians as the center of Christianity (even though Jesus' relatives, the *desposynoi*, continued to run the Pella Church). But despite the Jerusalem/Pella Church's fall from authority, the *Didache* was revered for centuries. It was quoted, often as Scripture, by church writers until the fifth century.

4. The Didache's status

When Athanasius, Patriarch of Alexandria, first pronounced the canonical list that we still use today in 367 AD, he listed the *Didache* and the

---

10   A large part of the Jerusalem Church was comprised of tradition-keeping Jewish Christians (i.e. observing the circumcision and kosher food rules of the Torah) who accepted Jesus as "God's servant" *(pahis)* but not as "the son of God" in a divine sense. Other Jewish Christians accepted Jesus as the Messiah, the Savior, and the Son of God. James the Just, head of the Jerusalem Church until his death in 62 AD, led a mixed Christian community and one of the themes of his open letter to all the Jewish Christians, the Epistle of James, was a call for peace and for an end to acrimony among Christians. The Jerusalem Church fled to Pella (on the Jordan River) in 66 AD and the tradition-keeping Jewish Christians predominated there and were later called Ebionites.

11   About 150 AD, pagan writer Lucian of Samosata, from eastern Syria, wrote *De morte Peregrini*. The work is a study of the religious quest of Peregrinus Proteus ("Proteus the Pilgrim"), a second-century seeker-after-truth who experimented with several religions and whose Christian phase occurred in Syria. Proteus committed suicide by immolating himself at the Olympics (hence the work's title, *The Death of a Pilgrim*). After discussing early Christian communism, Lucian goes on to say that "whenever there comes to these people a skilled deceiver, a man capable of situations, he becomes rich in a short time by misleading these simple people."

Shepherd of Hermas[12] as "supplements" to the New Testament, not part of the canon but valuable for instructing new converts. In 410 AD Rufinus of Aquileia, Jerome's rival, penned the same canonical list and listed the *Shepherd of Hermas* and the *Two Ways* (the first part of the *Didache*) as writings supplementing the New Testament.

But by 500 AD the *Didache* had lost its high status. It became a lost work in the Early Middle Ages and was forgotten for a thousand years -- until the discovery of the only surviving copy in a patriarch's library in Istanbul in 1873.[13] Its publication at the end of 1883 shocked biblical scholars and the general public. Scholars are still trying to determine its meaning and significance.

---

12 This work is universally called "the *Shepherd of Hermas*" in modern literature. Its original title was simply *The Shepherd*. There were many works by that name in antiquity and the ancients distinguished them by the name of the author. Both Greek and Latin indicate authorship with a genitive construction, rather than with a preposition. A less literal but more accurate translation would be "*The Shepherd* (written) by Hermas."

13 A Georgian translation from the Early Middle Ages was found in Istanbul in the 1920s. But it disappeared about 1930, before it could be examined by scholars.

CHAPTER 3

"Love Your Enemies"

1. *The Didache opens with a passage from The Sayings*

The *Didache* contains several quotations from *The Sayings of Our Lord*. The first and longest is the *interpolatio evangelica* near the beginning of the *Didache* (verses 1.3b-1.5). The *Didache's* opening words are: "There are two ways: the Way of life and the Way of Death, and the difference between the two ways is great. The Way of Life is this: *Thou shalt love the Lord thy Creator,* and secondly, *thy neighbor as thyself,* and *thou shalt do nothing to any man that thou wouldst not wish to be done to thyself.*" These are quotations from Deuteronomy 6:5, Leviticus 19:18, and perhaps Tobit 4:15 (in the Septuagint). Next it says,

> Now the teaching of these words is this: ³ᵇ*Bless those that curse you,* and pray for your enemies, and <u>fast for those that persecute you</u>; ³ᶜfor what merit is there if you love those that love you? Do not even the Gentiles do that? ³ᵈ*But love those that hate you,* and you will have no enemy.
>
> ⁴ᵃAbstain from physical and bodily cravings. ⁴ᵇIf someone strikes you on your right cheek, turn the other to him too, and you will be perfect. ⁴ᶜ<u>If anyone forces you to go one mile, go two miles with him</u>. ⁴ᵈIf anyone takes away your coat, give him your shirt too. ⁴ᵉ*If anyone takes from you what is yours, do not demand it back,* for you cannot.
>
> ⁵ᵃGive to everyone that asks you, and do not demand it back. ⁵ᵇFor the Father wishes that from His Own gifts should be given to all. ⁵ᶜBlessed is he who gives according to the commandment, for he is innocent. Woe to him who receives; for if a man receives because he is in need, he will be innocent; but he who receives when he is not in

need will stand trial, as to why he received and for what,
^{5d}and being put in prison he will be examined about what
he has done, and he will not come out of it until he pays
the last penny.[14]

This passage is remarkably similar to Matt 5:39-48 (in the Sermon on the Mount) and Luke 6:27-33 (in the Sermon on the Plain). Many biblical scholars have assumed it was based on them, and therefore call it the *interpolatio evangelica* (the gospel interpolation). I prefer to call it the "love your enemies" passage. In this passage, many verses that appear in Matthew and Luke are intricately interwoven to form a more succinct version of this passage than appears in either of those gospels. This close-knit material includes several clauses which are present in either Matthew or Luke, but not both.

For example, "fast for those that persecute you" and "if anyone forces you to go one mile, go two miles with him" (underlined above) are in Matthew but not in Luke, while "bless those that curse you," "love those that hate you" and "if anyone takes from you what is yours, do not demand it back" (given in italics above) are in Luke but not in Matthew. The material in "love your enemies" is interwoven in such a way that the passage could have served as the basis for either the Matthean or Lucan versions. How could this textual maze have come about? A better explanation is that "love your enemies" is a passage from *The Sayings* that was later used in writing the gospels of Matthew and Luke.

Additional evidence that "love your enemies" is a quotation is found in the fact that it is introduced with the statement "the teaching of these words is this." *The teaching is this* is a standard Greek and Latin phrase used to introduce a quotation or make certain transitions in the text, and indicates that the following material is taken from another source, although in antiquity quotations were often loose rather than exact. Let us recall the words used by the Barnabist to append the *Two Ways* after *Barnabas* 17: "Now let us pass to another lesson and teaching." The words *another lesson and teaching* indicate that a new source is being used by the Barnabist. Thus the phrase *the teaching is this* indicates that the *interpolatio* is a quotation. Further evidence comes from a Latin translation of the *Two Ways*, called the *Doctrina Apostolorum*. The *Doctrina* lacks verses 1.3 to 2.1 because it represents an earlier version of the *Two Ways*.

---

14 The following verse isn't part of the passage (1:6, *But of this it was also said, "Let your charity sweat in your hands until you know to whom to give"*). The words "but of this it was also said" indicate that it comes from a different source.

2. The Didache's Lord's Prayer comes from The Sayings

The second-longest quotation from Matthew's *Sayings* found in the *Didache* is the Lord's Prayer (*Did.* 8:2). Here's how the *Didache* gives it:

> And do not pray like the hypocrites, but pray
> thus as the Lord commanded in His gospel:
>> Our Father in Heaven,
>> Your Name be revered,
>> Your Kingdom come,
>> Your will be done on earth as it is done in Heaven.
>> Give us today our bread for the day,
>> and forgive us our debt, as we forgive our debtors;
>> and do not subject us to temptation,
>> but save us from the Evil One;
>> for Yours is the power and the glory forever!

There are only minor differences between the *Didache*'s Lord's Prayer and that found in Matt 6:9-13 and Luke 11:2-4. Most notable is the absence of the words "the kingdom" in Matthew's last line, which is also absent from the Coptic versions (Sahidic and Fayyumic), and the absence of the entire last line in Luke's version. Otherwise, the Greek texts are almost identical. Since "kingdom" is a favorite word of the Mattheist, it may be that "kingdom" was added by the Mattheist into canonical Matthew's Lord's Prayer, and that the *Didache* preserves the original wording given in *The Sayings*. Alternatively, it may be that Luke preserves the original wording of the Lord's Prayer given in *The Sayings* (based on *lectio brevior*, that the shorter reading is usually the authentic one) and that the final lines in the *Didache* and the Gospel of Matthew were added later.

Note, too, that *Did.* 8:2 introduces the Lord's Prayer with the injunction "neither pray ye as the hypocrites, but as the Lord commanded in His gospel, after this manner pray ye..." While Matthew's Lord's Prayer begins at 6:9, the *Didache*'s first clause (on hypocrites) has its Matthean counterpart a few verses earlier at 6:5 and this should also be recognized as *Sayings* material.

3. Other Sayings material in the Didache

There are a few other sayings of Jesus in the *Didache* that are likely from Matthew's *Sayings*. *Did.* 9:5b ("do not give dogs what is sacred") is identical with Matt 7:6. Next, *Did.* 11:7 forbids putting skeptical questions to a prophet who is speaking in the spirit: "for every sin shall be forgiven, but this sin shall not be forgiven." This parallels Matt 12:31, which states that every sin will be forgiven except blaspheming the Holy Spirit. Third, *Did.* 13:1-2 says that "every true prophet... is worthy of his food. Likewise a true teacher is himself worthy, like the laborer, of his food." Matt 10:10 says that "the workman is worthy of his meat" (also in Luke 10:7). And fourth, *Did.* 16:1, which begins the *Didache's* apocalyptic section, says "watch for your life... for ye know not the hour in which our Lord cometh." This verse also appears in the apocalyptic sections of Matthew and Mark (Matt 24:42 and Mk 13:33).

Sayings material used in the *Didache*

Did. 1:3b-1:5, the "Love Your Enemies" passage (also found in Matthew's Sermon on the Mount and Luke's Sermon on the Plain)

Did. 8:2, the Lord's Prayer (also found in Matthew's Semon on the Mount and Luke's Sermon on the Plain)

Did. 9:5b, "Do not give dogs what is sacred" (also found in Matt 7:6)

Did. 11:7, "For every sin shall be forgiven, but this sin shall not be forgiven" (also found in Matt 12:31)

Did. 13:1-2, "Every true prophet... is worthy of his food. Likewise a true teacher is himself worthy, like the laborer, of his food" (paralleled in Matt 10:10 and Luke 10:7)

Did. 16:1, "Watch for your life... for ye know not the hour in which our Lord cometh" (also found in Matt 24:42 and Mk 13:33)

Scholars usually say that the *Didache* took this material from the Gospel of Matthew, but in fact it came to the *Didache* directly from *The Sayings*, and was later incorporated into the Gospel of Matthew (along with most of *The Sayings*).

4. The Didache's "gospel" was The Sayings of Our Lord

Finally, the *Didache* refers to *the gospel* several times: *Did.* 8:2 introduces the Lord's Prayer with the words "Pray thus as the Lord commanded in His Gospel"; 11:3 says "...follow the rule of the Gospel"; 15:3 says "Do not reprove one another in wrath, but in peace as you find it in the Gospel"; and 15:4 says "Offer your prayers and do your alms and all your acts as you find it in the Gospel of our Lord." That gospel was Matthew's *Sayings*.

CHAPTER 4

The Gospel of Mark

1. Background on the Gospel of Mark

In the mid or late 50s the Apostle Peter went to Rome to preach and evangelize. It appears that Peter only spoke Aramaic and that his audience was limited at first.[15] A couple of years later John Mark, who had been a companion of Paul a few years earlier, went to Rome and served as Peter's interpreter. Peter was martyred in the great persecution of Nero in 64 AD. Mark was greatly affected by Peter's death, but remained in Italy for a while longer.[16] Mark probably wrote his gospel in 65 AD, putting down everything he could remember Peter saying about Jesus' ministry (although it is also possible that Mark had been writing down Peter's account for some time).

LITERARY SOURCES FOR THE GOSPEL OF MARK

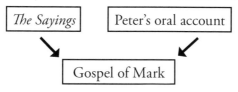

Such is the traditional account. But in addition to his memory of what Peter had said, Mark also had before him a copy of *The Sayings of Our Lord*.[17] This provided much material for his gospel, in which he combines Peter's memoirs with those of Matthew. Jerome, in his

---

15   In this case, Peter's amanuensis Silvanus would likely have been translating Peter's first epistle from Aramaic to Greek as he was taking dictation from Peter.

16   Mark later went to Alexandria, Egypt, the site of a large Jewish community, and Egypt's Coptic Church has always regarded him as its founder.

17   Probably not *The Sayings* in Aramaic, but one of the Greek translations that Papias mentions, because it is unlikely that Mark would have mistranslated *gamla* (discussed below) since Aramaic was his first language.

Commentary on Matthew (written about 405 AD), states that Mark "set forth with great care all the things that he had heard his master preaching, but not in order." It is not clear what Jerome meant by "in order" -- in chronological order? in Peter's order? in Matthew or Luke's order? or in some other order?

2. The Sayings provided the Gospel of Mark's framework

The Sayings may have provided Mark with some of the framework for his gospel. For example, Epiphanius states in *Panarion* (28.5) that Matthew's Hebrew gospel was missing the genealogy and other material (presumably including the nativity and childhood narratives),[18] which are not present in Mark's gospel. And Epiphanius states in *Panarion* (30.13.6) that the Hebrew gospel begins this way:

> It happened in the days of Herod, King of Judea, when the high-priest was Caiaphas, that there came a certain man, John by name, baptizing the baptism of conversion in the Jordan River. It is said concerning him that he was of the family of Aaron the Priest, the son of Zachariah and Elisabeth. And all went out unto him...

Mark opens his gospel by quoting an Old Testament prophecy (Mal 3:1, Isa 40:3), then immediately introduces John the Baptist baptizing in the Jordan River:

> [4]John did baptize in the wilderness, and preach the baptism of repentance for the remission of sins. [5]And there went out unto him all the land of Judea, and they of Jerusalem, and were all baptized of him in the river of Jordan, confessing their sins... [9]And it came to pass in those days, that Jesus came from Nazareth of Galilee, and was baptized of John in Jordan.[19]

---

18 *Panarion* 28.5 reads (in Latin) "Matthaei enim Evangelio, non integro, sed ex parte duntaxat utuntur, nimirum propter genealogiam, quae eius est carnis propria, quod quidem Evangelii testimonium afferunt, atque ita praedicant" (given in Migne, PG 41, col. 383). Migne's note on Irenaeus relating to this describes Matthew's Hebrew gospel as "non integro, sed prioribus duobus capitibus mutilo, aliisque in locis depravato" (PG 7, pt. 1, col. 884, n. 85, referencing *Panarion* 30.13).

19 It is interesting that further down in that same passage (Epiphanius's quotation of the Hebrew Gospel's account of John's baptism of Jesus) it says (after the descent of the dove and the voice from heaven): "and suddenly a great light shone about that place." This is surely the origin of the "great light" verse that occurs in several early copies of canonical

The similarity between the two beginnings is considerable. Did Mark draw his opening from that in *The Sayings*? Although it would be interesting to know how the Apostle Peter used to begin the story of Jesus' ministry, it is likely that this and much else in Mark's gospel were patterned after *The Sayings*. (In *Panarion* 30.13 Epiphanius quotes additional material from the beginning of *The Sayings* which connects with the accounts of John's ministry and Jesus' baptism in the synoptic gospels. This material is given at the end of chapter 8.) Let us look at another example.

3. The Story of the Rich Young Ruler

One of the incidents in *The Sayings*, the story of the Rich Young Ruler, was recorded by the early third-century theologian Origen, who was head of the Catechetical School in Alexandria, Egypt. Origen says in his commentary *On Matthew* (15.14) that the *Gospel according to the Hebrews* (a later name for *The Sayings*) says the following:

> "Another of the rich men," it says, "said to Him, Master, what good must I do to live? He said to him: Man, do the Law and the Prophets. He answered Him: I did. He said to him: Go, sell all that you possess and divide it among the poor and come, follow Me. But the rich man began to scratch his head and it did not please him. And the Lord said to him: Why do you say, I did the Law and the Prophets? Since it is written in the Law: Love your neighbor as yourself? and behold many of your brothers, sons of Abraham, are covered with dung, dying from hunger, and your house is filled with many good things, and absolutely nothing goes out of it to them. And He turned and said to Simon, His disciple sitting with Him: Simon, son of Jona, it is easier for a camel to pass through the eye of a needle than for a rich man into the kingdom of Heaven."[20]

Matthew, as well as in Justin Martyr and the *Diatessaron*. It is likely that a number of other variant readings in early copies of the synoptic gospels also derive from material in *The Sayings*.

20   There are two elements in the last verse which are not likely to have been in *The Sayings*: 1) It is generally accepted that the word *camel [gamal]* in the "camel passing through the eye of a needle" is a misunderstanding of the Aramaic word *gamla*, which means *rope* or *knot*. This translation error likely happened early on, and may have been in the Greek version of *The Sayings* used by Mark. 2) The phrase "the kingdom of Heaven" is probably an error

Now let's look at this passage as given in Mark 10:17-25:

> [17]And when He was gone forth into the way, there came one running, and kneeled to Him, and asked Him, Good Master, what shall I do that I may inherit eternal life? [18]And Jesus said unto him, Why callest thou Me good, there is none good but One, that is, God. [19]Thou knowest the commandments, Do not commit adultery, Do not kill, Do not steal, Do not bear false witness, Defraud not, Honor thy father and mother. [20]And he answered and said unto Him, Master, all these have I observed from my youth. [21]Then Jesus beholding him loved him, and said unto him, One thing thou lackest: go thy way, sell whatsoever thou hast, and give to the poor, and thou shalt have treasure in heaven: and come, take up the cross,[21] and follow Me. [22]And he was sad at that saying, and went away grieved: for he had great possessions. [23]And Jesus looked round about, and saith unto His disciples, How hardly shall they that have riches enter into the kingdom of God! [24]And the disciples were astonished at His words. But Jesus answereth again, and saith unto them, Children, how hard is it for them that trust in riches to enter into the kingdom of God! [25]It is easier for a camel to go through the eye of a needle, than for a rich man to enter into the kingdom of God.

Mark's version of this incident ends with several more verses that are not given in Origen's extract (the discussion about who could be saved). Since it is unknown whether there was comparable material at the end of *The Sayings'* account which Origen omitted, the present work will consider the story to end with the words "than for a rich man to enter into the kingdom of God."

---

for "the kingdom of God," which is how it is given in Mark 10:25 and Matt 19:24. This is contrary to the normal usage of the Mattheist, who favors the expression "the kingdom of Heaven." Since the last verse was (and is) very well-known, Origen may have converted its "kingdom" phrase into the canonical Matthew form with which he was familiar.

21   There is uncertainty about the status of the words "take up the cross." Of the three major fourth-century manuscripts, it is present in the Codex Alexandrinus (A), but absent from the Codex Sinaiticus (‭א‬) and the Codex Vaticanus (B). It is present in the Textus Receptus and the King James Bible, but has been omitted from most twentieth-century versions. Some textual scholars say it was taken from Mark 8:34. The present writer believes it is authentic because *it sounds like* something Mark's Gospel would say.

A Key Verse

The Sayings of Our Lord contained an account of Jesus' encounter with a young man known as "the rich young ruler," in which the young man asked Jesus what he needed to do in order to obtain eternal life. The way the Apostle Matthew remembered it, Jesus told the rich young man, "Sell all that you possess and divide it among the poor and come, follow Me." This incident also appears in the Gospel of Mark, but in Mark Jesus says, "Sell whatsoever thou hast, and give to the poor, and thou shalt have treasure in heaven: and come, take up the cross, and follow Me." Mark's Gospel adds the commandment to *take up the cross,* and states that in giving to the poor, the young man *will have treasure in heaven.* Mark's version has a spiritual depth that is lacking in *The Sayings,* because Mark wrote with the guidance of the Holy Spirit.

---

4. Mark presents Jesus' teachings better than The Sayings

While there are many differences between these two versions (such as Mark's addition of Jesus' question about being called good, Mark's omission of Jesus' accusation to the rich young man that he was giving nothing to the poor, and Mark's expansion of Jesus' audience from Simon to the disciples generally), there are two significant ones: 1) Mark's account explains that if the rich young man gives his possessions to the poor he will have treasure in heaven, which *The Sayings* did not do; and 2) Mark's account adds that the rich young man must also "take up the cross" (undergo deprivation and persecution) in order to follow Jesus.

The changes that Mark makes present Jesus' teachings more fully than *The Sayings* does. *The Sayings* records Jesus' advice to the rich young man to give his wealth to the poor without explaining its significance and spiritual reward, and lacks Jesus' statement that personal sacrifice is required in order to be one of His followers. *The Sayings* account is spiritually thin, while Mark's version is eye-to-eye with Jesus. It is likely that throughout *The Sayings* events were recounted with little or no explanation of their real significance. Mark, on the other hand, wrote with the guidance of the Holy Spirit.

The Gospel of Mark also has a high Christology. Mark states repeatedly that Jesus is the Son of God (Mk 1:1, 3:11, 5:7, 14:61, 15:39), and the Parable of the Wicked Vineyard Tenants in Mark 12 presents Jesus as the Son of God. Christ's atonement for our sins is expressed in a single verse spoken by Jesus about a week before the Crucifixion (Mk 10:45, "the Son of Man came not to be ministered unto, but to minister, and to give His life a ransom for many"). Mark's theological statements are few and brief, consistent with his terse writing style, but set forth a high Christology and soteriology.

5. The Gospel of Mark's original name

Finally, Mark likely called his gospel simply *The Gospel of Jesus Christ*. The word *gospel*, not used in the title of *The Sayings*, had been used by Paul for at least fifteen years and had gained acceptance as the general term for Jesus' teachings. And, of course, the words "according to Mark" were added by a later copyist to distinguish it from the following gospels, those of Luke and (canonical) Matthew.

6. Conclusion

In conclusion, the Gospel of Mark, the first of the four canonical gospels, was based on both *The Sayings* and on Peter's oral account of Jesus' ministry. *The Sayings* also provided the Gospel of Mark with its basic framework. However, Mark's gospel is far superior to *The Sayings* because it was inspired by the Holy Spirit and presents Jesus' teachings more fully than *The Sayings* does.

CHAPTER 5

The Gospel of Luke

1. Backround on the Gospel of Luke

The Gospel according to Luke was composed, according to tradition, by the physician Luke, who was an associate of Paul and accompanied him on some of his journeys. He created his gospel in (or not long after) 70 AD (based on his knowledge of the Roman army's encirclement of Jerusalem, described in Lk 21:20), and wrote the Acts of the Apostles some time after that. Luke employed several sources for his work, including *The Sayings*, the Gospel of Mark, and no doubt the testimony of many long-time Christians -- all given in very polished writing.[22] He wrote with the guidance of the Holy Spirit.

LITERARY SOURCES FOR THE GOSPEL OF LUKE

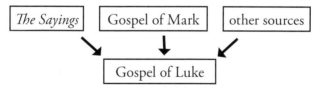

---

22   Half of the Gospel of Luke consists of parables that are unique to Luke (most are given in 9:51-18:14), called Special Luke. Some scholars feel there is evidence that this large block of material was based on a Hebrew source. Much of this evidence is given in James R. Edwards's 2009 work *The Hebrew Gospel and the Development of the Synoptic Tradition* (esp. pp. 131-148 and 185), which addresses Papias's statement. Unfortunately Edwards argues, as the core of his book, that this is proof that Matthew's *Sayings* was written in Hebrew and that *The Sayings* was the primary or sole source for Special Luke (pp. 260-62). This is remarkable since all the *Sayings* material quoted by early Christian writers occurs in the general synoptic tradition -- the Triple Tradition (material common to Matthew, Mark, and Luke) and the Double Tradition (material common to Matthew and Luke) -- never in Special Luke. If Special Luke was based on a Hebrew source (which it may or may not have been), that source was not *The Sayings*.

2. Luke's John-the-Baptist passage based on The Sayings

Luke began his gospel with a genealogy and a nativity narrative given to prove that Jesus was the promised Savior-Messiah. Immediately after the genealogy and nativity, Luke tells the story of John the Baptist, which was *The Sayings'* opening passage. Let's take another look at how *The Sayings* begins:

> It happened in the days of Herod, King of Judea, during the time when Caiaphas was high-priest, that a certain John came, baptizing the baptism of conversion in the Jordan River. It is said concerning him that he was of the family of Aaron the Priest, the son of Zachariah and Elisabeth. And all went out unto him...

Luke's story of John the Baptist in chapter 3 is very similar:

> [2]Annas and Caiaphas being the high-priests, the Word of God came unto John the son of Zacharias in the wilderness. [3]And he came into all the country about Jordan, preaching the baptism of repentance for the remission of sins.

But before that Luke puts into his nativity story John the Baptist's parents, Zachariah and Elisabeth, who appear in *The Sayings'* opening. Here's what Luke says in chapter 1:

> [36]And, behold, thy cousin Elisabeth, she hath also conceived a son... [39]And Mary arose in those days, and went into the hill country with haste, into a city of Judah, [40]and entered into the house of Zecharias, and saluted Elisabeth. [41]...when Elisabeth heard the salutation of Mary, the babe leaped in her womb, and Elisabeth was filled with the Holy Ghost... [67]And his father Zacharias... prophesied, saying... [68]Blessed be the Lord God of Israel, for He hath visited and redeemed His people...

Although Luke's tale of Zacharias and Elisabeth was likely suggested by *The Sayings'* reference to them, *The Sayings* itself appears to have only mentioned their names, without telling their important story or relating its significance. Luke's narrative, on the other hand, is dynamic and projects the auspiciousness of John's coming ministry, declaring it the fulfillment of prophecy. Luke's account was inspired by the Holy Spirit.

SPECIAL LUKE

About half of the Gospel of Luke consists of material that is unique to Luke and is not found in the other two synoptic gospels. This material, called Special Luke, is not part of the general synoptic tradition, and constitutes almost all of Luke 9:51-18:14. Special Luke consists largely of parables, such as the Parable of the Good Samaritan, the Rich Fool, the Prodigal Son, the Rich Man and Lazarus, etc. It is unknown whether Luke obtained this material from those who had heard Jesus speak, or from one of the earlier writings mentioned in his prologue (1:1-3).

3. *The Rich Young Ruler*

Now let's look at how Luke deals with another passage from *The Sayings*: the story of the Rich Young Ruler that we examined in the previous section on Mark. Here's how this passage is given in Luke 18:18-25:

> [18]And a certain ruler asked Him, saying, Good Master, what shall I do to inherit eternal life? [19]And Jesus said unto him, Why callest thou Me good? None is good save One, that is God. [20]Thou knowest the commandments, Do not commit adultery, Do not kill, Do not steal, Do not bear false witness, Honor thy father and thy mother. [21]And he said, All these have I kept from my youth up. [22]Now when Jesus heard these things, He said unto him, Yet lackest thou one thing: sell all that thou hast, and distribute unto the poor, and thou shalt have treasure in heaven: and come, follow Me. [23]And when he heard this, he was very sorrowful; for he was very rich. [24]And when Jesus saw that he was very sorrowful, He said, How hardly shall they that have riches enter into the kingdom of God! [25]For it is easier for a camel to go through a needle's eye, than for a rich man to enter into the kingdom of God.

Since there are two earlier accounts of the Rich Young Ruler, we need to compare Luke's version with both of them. Luke based his version primarily on that of Mark. He took four things from Mark: 1) Jesus' question about being called good; 2) the citation of several of the Ten Commandments; 3) the statement about having treasure in heaven; and 4) the expansion of Jesus' audience from Simon to the disciples generally.

He also omitted, as Mark had, Jesus' accusation to the rich young man that he had not given to the poor.

But Luke followed *The Sayings* in one thing: his opening words are simple ("a certain ruler asked Him..."), just as *The Sayings'* opening words are ("another of the rich men said to him..."). Mark, on the other hand, expands this to "and when He was gone forth into the way, there came one running, and kneeled to Him, and asked Him..." Mark probably didn't invent the actions of Jesus walking in the street and someone running up to Him and kneeling before Him. These details probably came from Peter, whose story-telling style may be the source of Mark's usually fast-paced narrative. (Peter may also have been the source for the other Marcan additions listed above, and the Holy Spirit surely guided Mark throughout.) Luke rejected Mark's expanded opening and followed that of *The Sayings*. Luke also identified the young man as *a rich man*, just as *The Sayings* identified him as *a certain ruler*. Mark on the other hand, merely says *(some)one*, without identifying him as a member of the upper class. Luke thus based his version of the Rich Young Ruler on both *The Sayings* and the Gospel of Mark.

4. *"Love your enemies"*

Let us now turn to another segment in Luke that comes from *The Sayings*, the "love your enemies" passage that also appears in the *Didache*'s introduction. Here's how it's written in *The Sayings* (with an improvised verse-numbering system):

> ^{A}Bless those that curse you, and pray for your enemies, and fast for those that persecute you; ^{B}for what merit is there if you love those that love you? Do not even the Gentiles do that? ^{B2}But love those that hate you, and you will have no enemy.
>
> ^{B3}Abstain from physical and bodily cravings. ^{C}If someone strikes you on your right cheek, turn the other to him too, and you will be perfect. ^{C2}If anyone forces you to go one mile, go two miles with him. ^{D}If anyone takes away your coat, give him your shirt too. ^{E}If anyone takes from you what is yours, do not demand it back, for you cannot.
>
> ^{F}Give to everyone that asks you, and do not demand it back. ^{F2}For the Father wishes that from His Own gifts should be given to all. ^{F3}Blessed is he who gives according

to the commandment, for he is innocent. Woe to him who receives; for if a man receives because he is in need, he will be innocent; but he who receives when he is not in need will stand trial, as to why he received and for what, ꟳ⁴and being put in prison he will be examined about what he has done, and he will not come out of it until he pays the last penny.

In the above verse-numbering system, the letters A-F are assigned to verses that also appear in Luke's version of "love your enemies." The designations B2, B3, C2, F2, F3 and F4 are used for those verses that don't appear in it. Here's Luke's version of "love your enemies" (Luke 6:27-32), using the above verse-numbering system:

> ᴬLove your enemies, do good to them which hate you, bless them that curse you, and pray for them which despitefully use you. ᶜAnd unto him that smiteth thee on the one cheek, offer also the other. ᴰAnd him that taketh away thy cloak, forbid not to take thy coat also. ꟳGive to every man that asketh of thee. ᴱAnd of him that taketh away thy goods, ask them not again. ᴳᵒˡᵈᵉⁿ ᴿᵘˡᵉAnd as ye would have that men should do to you, do ye also to them likewise. ᴮFor if ye love them which love you, what thank have ye? for sinners also love those that love them.

The two passages are closely related, both in contents and order. In *The Sayings*, the order of verses is ABCDEF. Luke's order is ACDFE-GR-B. This moves the second verse to the end and interpolates the Golden Rule just before it. He also condenses B2 ("love those that hate you, and you will have no enemy") into "love your enemies" and places it at the beginning of verse A (which is appropriate because it is the theme of the passage). Luke's passage consists almost entirely of *Sayings* material, in a very similar order. Luke contains no expansions or additional material, except the Golden Rule. This is striking, especially when one considers that *The Sayings* probably contained the Golden Rule nearby,[23] which would mean that

---

23 The Golden Rule was likely in *The Sayings,* and near "love your enemies", because it is in the Gospel of Matthew, near the end of the Sermon on the Mount (Matt 7:12). British theologian Thomas W. Manson wrote in 1949 that the different versions of the Golden Rule found in Matt 7:12 and Lk 6:31 could be easily explained by the presence of a certain Aramaic phrase (kma de) in the original text. Manson states that "there is a sufficient number of such translation variants to justify the belief that [the source writing] was originally an Aramaic document and that in Mt. and Lk. we have two renderings of it" (*The Sayings of Jesus,* p. 19).

Luke's passage actually has no additions. But notice that Luke's version of verse B changes *Gentiles* to *sinners* to avoid offending the Gentiles who were the majority of Paul's followers.

Notice also that Luke's version of "love your enemies" is a better statement of that theme than *The Sayings'* version is. In order to achieve this, Luke omits verses B3, F3, and F4, which don't concern loving one's enemies. But he also omits verses C2, and F2, which do concern loving one's enemies, and his reason for doing so is unclear. Nevertheless, Luke's version of "love your enemies" hits deep into one's heart and dovetails with another passage in his gospel, the Parable of the Good Samaritan. The Parable of the Good Samaritan tells the story of how a wounded Jew is cared for by a Samaritan, a group the Jews considered their enemies -- a story of loving your enemy. "Love your enemies" and the Parable of the Good Samaritan are clear evidence that Luke wrote his gospel with the guidance of the Holy Spirit.

5. The Gospel of Luke's name

Finally, it is likely that Luke called his gospel *The Gospel of Jesus Christ according to Luke* in order to distinguish it from that of Mark, which was probably still called simply *The Gospel of Jesus Christ*. Mark's name was likely added to his gospel at a later time. However, this explanation of the names of the first canonical gospels is speculative, since no copies of these gospels survive from the mid-first century.

6. Conclusion

In conclusion, three main points stand out: First, that Luke used *The Sayings* in composing his gospel. Second, that *The Sayings* falls short of the Gospel of Luke in presenting Jesus' message. And third, that the Gospel of Luke is inspired Scripture.

CHAPTER 6

The Gospel of Matthew

1. Background on the Gospel of Matthew

Matthew's *Sayings of Our Lord* was written about 40 AD. The *Didache* was put together about 60 AD. The Gospel of Mark, which was unknown to the Didachist, was probably written soon after Peter's death in 64 AD. The Gospel of Luke was written about 70 AD. The Gospel of Matthew was probably written about 75 AD or a few years later.

LITERARY SOURCES FOR THE GOSPEL OF MATTHEW

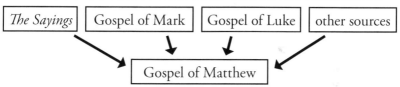

2. The Mattheist

The author of the Gospel of Matthew was an educated Greek-speaking Christian, whom scholars call the Mattheist.[24] The Mattheist was probably multilingual, possibly of Jewish descent, and may have lived in Antioch. Because the Gospel of Matthew is so complete and so perfectly constructed, many modern scholars, such as Krister Stendahl, believe that it was the product of a *school* -- that is, a group of experts that worked together in developing its teachings. The present writer believes that it was the product of one man, who was guided by the Holy Spirit in crafting his gospel to perfection.

The Mattheist was well-versed both in Christian teachings and in the Old Testament, and was possibly a church elder or a scribe for the

---

24   See George D. Kilpatrick, *The Origins of the Gospel according to St. Matthew* (1946).

local Christian community. It is likely that he didn't produce the Gospel of Matthew on his own initiative, but was entrusted with the task by the church leadership. The primary purpose was to produce an account of Jesus' ministry that emphasizes Jesus' fulfillment of Old Testament messianic prophecy, and His mission to both Jews and Gentiles.

The gospel was intended for use in church services, including the liturgy, and was produced primarily out of materials already in use in church services and teaching meetings. These included *The Sayings*, the Gospels of Mark and Luke, information about Jesus' birth and childhood, a list of Old Testament messianic prophecies fulfilled by Him, and other materials. The project was primarily a revision of *The Sayings*, material from which played a major part in early Christian worship services, and the finished work was called the Gospel of Matthew for that reason.

3. "Love your enemies" -- the text of Matt 5:39-48

Let's look at how the Mattheist re-wrote some of the material in *The Sayings*. Here is the quotation from *The Sayings* given in the *Didache* (the "love your enemies" passage):

> [3b]Bless those that curse you, and pray for your enemies, and fast for those that persecute you; [3c]for what merit is there if you love those that love you? Do not even the Gentiles do that? [3d]But love those that hate you, and you will have no enemy.
>
> [4a]Abstain from physical and bodily cravings. [4b]If someone strikes you on your right cheek, turn the other to him too, and you will be perfect. [4c]If anyone forces you to go one mile, go two miles with him. [4d]If anyone takes away your coat, give him your shirt too. [4e]If anyone takes from you what is yours, do not demand it back, for you cannot.
>
> [5a]Give to everyone that asks you, and do not demand it back. [5b]For the Father wishes that from His Own gifts should be given to all. [5c]Blessed is he who gives according to the commandment, for he is innocent. Woe to him who receives; for if a man receives because he is in need, he will be innocent; but he who receives when he is not in need will stand trial, as to why he received and for what, [5d]and being put in prison he will be examined about what

he has done, and he will not come out of it until he pays the last penny.

Now let's look at Matt 5:39-48:

> [39]But I say unto you, That ye resist not evil: but whosoever shall smite thee on thy right cheek, turn to him the other also. [40]And if any man will sue thee at the law, and take away thy coat, let him have thy cloak also. [41]And whosoever shall compel thee to go a mile, go with him twain. [42]Give to him that asketh thee, and from him that would borrow of thee turn not thou away. [43]Ye have heard that it hath been said, Thou shalt love thy neighbor, and hate thine enemy. [44]But I say unto you, Love your enemies, bless them that curse you, do good to them that hate you, and pray for them which despitefully use you, and persecute you; [45]That ye may be the children of your Father which is in Heaven: for He maketh His sun to rise on the evil and on the good, and sendeth rain on the just and on the unjust. [46]For if ye love them which love you, what reward have ye? do not even the publicans the same? [47]And if ye salute your brethren only, what do ye more than others? do not even the publicans so? [48]Be ye therefore perfect, even as your Father which is in Heaven is perfect.

4. "Love your enemies" -- zeroing in on Matt 5:43-44

Now let's see what the Mattheist does with the first few verses of the *Sayings* quotation. *Did.* 1:3b (which I will call *Sayings* 1:3b for convenience sake) says *Bless those that curse you, and pray for your enemies, and fast for those that persecute you.* Luke had introduced this commandment with the words "love your enemies." The Mattheist expands this introduction by having Jesus say in the preceding verse (Matt 5:43) "Ye have heard that it hath been said, *Thou shalt love thy neighbor and hate thy enemy*, but I say unto you, love your enemies..." "Love thy neighbor and hate thy enemy" is based on a commandment on the first page of the Essenes' *Community Rule*, which the Mattheist was sure his audience had heard. "Love your enemies" was Jesus' answer to the problem of hatred. And both Luke and Matthew place it at the beginning of this teaching section.

Sayings 1:3b: *Bless those that curse you, and pray for your enemies, and fast for those that persecute you* is re-written in Matt 5:44 as *Love your enemies, bless them that curse you, do good to them that hate you, and pray for them which despitefully use you, and persecute you.*[25] In this the Mattheist switches the order of the first two clauses, adds another clause between *The Sayings*' second and third clauses, and makes changes in wording that expand the intent of the *Sayings* verse.

Specifically, the Mattheist adds the commandment to *do good to them that hate you. The Sayings*' instructions to *bless, pray for* and *fast for* are things that don't involve confronting or having direct contact with those who oppose you. It's the easy way of handling the situation. The Mattheist adds the commandment to *do good to them*, ensuring that they know that you love them rather than hate them. This is a difficult thing to do because it involves humbling yourself, and replacing love of self with love for others. It goes beyond turning the other cheek, carrying a Roman soldier's pack for a mile, allowing your coat to be appropriated, and giving away things that are asked for, in all of which you are probably an impersonal victim. This involves doing something good for someone who *hates* you, and that's much more difficult. But it's what Jesus wants us to do. The Mattheist has voiced a higher level of obedience and service desired by the Lord: *to love your neighbor as yourself in spite of his bad treatment of you.*

5. "Love your enemies" -- the rest of Matt 5:39-49

The following sub-verse in *The Sayings* (1:3c) says *For what merit is there if you love those that love you? Do not even the Gentiles do that?* This is re-written in Matt 5:46 as *For if ye love them which love you, what reward have ye? do not even the publicans the same?* Here the Mattheist has put another verse (Matt 5:45, which has no counter-part in the *Sayings* quotation) between *Sayings* 1:3b and 1:3c. In addition, in *The Sayings* the Gentiles -- who make up a large part of the Mattheist's target audience -- are referred to as a detestable group of people. The Mattheist therefore changes *Gentiles* to *publicans* (tax-collectors), a group that everybody hates. Luke had re-written it with the word *sinners.*

The sub-verse after the next in *The Sayings* -- (4a) *Abstain from physical and bodily cravings* -- has no counter-part in the Gospel of Matthew. (1 Peter 2:11 has a short parallel to *abstain from physical and bodily cravings,*

---

25 This is the wording of the King James Bible, which the present writer accepts as true. Most textual critics reject the authenticity of much of this verse, and many modern Bible versions translate it differently.

but this probably derives not from *The Sayings*, but either from Peter's memory of it as something Jesus used to say, or from its currency as one of the sayings of the Apostolic Church.)

The next sub-verse in *The Sayings* -- (4b) *If someone strikes you on your right cheek, turn the other to him too, and you will be perfect* -- is paralleled in Matt 5:39, *but whosoever shall smite thee on thy right cheek, turn to him the other also.* The Mattheist omits *and you will be perfect* from the end of "turn the other cheek" because he uses *perfect* in 5:48. There he modifies Luke 6:36 ("be ye therefore merciful, as your Father also is merciful") by substituting *perfect* for *merciful*. This yields "be ye therefore perfect, even as your Father which is in heaven is perfect," which is an appropriate way of ending that section. (See chapter 9 for a fuller discussion of Luke 6:36.)

The Mattheist reverses the order of *The Sayings'* next two sub-verses, 4c (on going the extra mile) and 4d (on giving your coat and cloak), and changes *if anyone takes away your coat,* to *if any man will sue thee at the law and take away thy coat.* Presumably this relates to repaying a debt.

And skipping down, *Sayings* 5d -- *and being put in prison he will be examined about what he has done, and he will not come out of it until he pays the last penny* -- is transformed by the Mattheist into Matt 5:25b-26, *and the judge will deliver thee to the officer, and thou shalt be cast into prison. Verily I say unto thee, thou shalt by no means come out thence, till thou hast paid the uttermost farthing.* Here the Mattheist has changed the context. *The Sayings* is talking about someone accepting charity when he isn't in need, while Matt 5:25-26 is talking about a debtor being brought to court by his creditor. The Mattheist has changed the context of the incident in order to use it as an illustration for his previous verses (Matt 5:23-24) on the need for reconciliation. In doing this, the Mattheist has upgraded the meaning of the verse (from not abusing charity to reconciliation with your fellow man).

The relationship between Matthew's "love your enemies" passage and that in the Gospel of Luke is very close. If we had used the "ABCDEF verse-numbering system" (used in the previous section on Luke) to see how the Mattheist re-orders the verses in "love your enemies" (*vis-a-vis* the order in *The Sayings*), we would see that the order of verses in Matthew is CDFAB -- very similar to Luke's order, ACDFE-GR-B. In addition, the Mattheist uses the phrase "love your enemies" (absent in *The Sayings*) at the beginning of verse A, which he takes from Luke. The Mattheist thus used both *The Sayings* and the Gospel of Luke when he created his version of "love your enemies."

The Composition of
The Sermon on the Mount

Jesus may have preached the Sermon on the Mount in 27 AD. The Apostle Matthew wrote *The Sayings of Our Lord* about 40 AD, and recorded his memory of the Sermon in it, most of which has not survived. The *Didache,* written about 60 AD, opens with a quotation from the Sermon's "love your enemies" passage, taken from *The Sayings* and gives a version of the Lord's Prayer that may be the same as what *The Sayings* recorded. Mark did not include the Sermon on the Mount in his gospel, written about 65 AD. The Gospel of Luke, written about 70 AD, presents an account, called the Sermon on the Plain, which is probably very close to that given in *The Sayings.* The Gospel of Matthew, written by the Mattheist about 75 AD, gives an expanded version of the Sermon. The last part of Matthew's Sermon on the Mount probably includes material taken from *The Sayings' logia* section.

---

6. *The Rich Young Ruler*

Now let's look at how the Mattheist deals with another passage from *The Sayings*: the story of the Rich Young Ruler that we examined in the previous sections on Mark and Luke. Here's how this passage is given in Matt 19:16-24:

> [16]And, behold, one came and said unto Him, Good Master, what good thing shall I do, that I may have eternal life? [17]And He said unto him, Why callest thou Me good? there is none good but One, that is, God: but if thou wilt enter into life, keep the commandments. [18]He saith unto Him, Which? Jesus said, Thou shalt do no murder, Thou shalt not commit adultery, Thou shalt not steal, Thou shalt not bear false witness, [19]Honor thy father and thy mother: and, Thou shalt love thy neighbor as thyself. [20]The young man saith unto Him, All these things I have kept from my youth up: what lack I yet? [21]Jesus said unto him, If thou wilt be perfect, go and sell that thou hast, and give to the poor, and thou shalt have treasure in heaven: and come and follow Me. [22]But when the young man heard that saying, he went away sorrowful: for he had great possessions. [23]Then said Jesus unto His disciples, Verily I

> say unto you, that a rich man shall hardly enter into the
> kingdom of heaven. [24]And again I say unto you, It is easier
> for a camel to go through the eye of a needle, than for a
> rich man to enter into the kingdom of God.

Since there are three earlier accounts of the Rich Young Ruler (*The Sayings*, Mark, and Luke), we need to compare the Mattheist's version with all three of them. The Mattheist based his version primarily on that of Mark, agreeing with Mark (over Luke) in several places. However, the Mattheist followed Luke and *The Sayings* in one thing: his opening words are simple ("and, behold, one came unto Him and said..."), as are the opening words of *The Sayings* ("another of the rich men said to him...") and Luke ("and a certain ruler asked Him..."). The Mattheist rejected Mark's expanded opening and followed those of Luke and *The Sayings*.

For the rest of his account, however, the Mattheist follows Mark. The Mattheist's major change here is that after repeating Mark's abbreviated Ten Commandments, he adds "love your neighbor as yourself" (from Leviticus 19:18), which neither *The Sayings* nor Mark give. The addition of "love your neighbor as yourself" is significant because it is given as one of Jesus' key teachings in Matt 22 (shown by His following statement that "all the Law and the Prophets" hang on the two Great Commandments).

7. How the Mattheist transformed Sayings material

These two quotations from *The Sayings* in early Christian literature ("love your enemies" and the story of the Rich Young Ruler), although preserved randomly, illustrate some of the ways in which the Mattheist transformed *The Sayings* into the Gospel of Matthew. The first is that the Mattheist re-arranged the material in *The Sayings*, re-writing it in accordance with his needs, and at times adding and removing material.

(The present writer believes that the Mattheist preserved almost all of *The Sayings* in the Gospel of Matthew, or at least as much as possible -- one story that didn't make it will be considered later. In line with this, it's possible that when the Mattheist finished constructing his gospel, he collected all or many of the sayings he hadn't used and added them into the Sermon of the Mount, especially in Matt 7:6-7:16, in order not to discard them.)

The second way in which the Mattheist changed *The Sayings* is that when he expanded or re-wrote *Sayings* material he usually did so in order to present Jesus' teachings more fully. In re-writing the "love your enemies" passage, the Mattheist added the commandment to "be children of your Father which is in heaven" (Matt 5:45), and he expanded the story of the Rich Young Ruler to include "love your neighbor as yourself" (the Second Great Commandment). These are statements about believers' relations with God and our fellow man that are not found in the *Sayings* material, but are key teachings of Jesus. The Holy Spirit guided the Mattheist in writing these passages, and in writing his entire gospel. (The Gospel of Matthew is perfect beyond human ability!)

8. The Gospel of Matthew's name

Finally, the words "according to Matthew" were probably included in the title by the Mattheist (rather than using his own name) both because Luke had done the same thing, and in order to declare that the work was a faithful presentation of *The Sayings'* contents. In addition, it is likely that at that time Mark's gospel was still entitled simply *The Gospel according to Jesus Christ*, and that the words "according to Mark" were subsequently added in response to the appearance of "according to Luke" and "according to Matthew" in the titles of those two gospels.

9. Conclusion

In conclusion, with the guidance of the Holy Spirit the Mattheist re-wrote material in *The Sayings* in ways that transformed Matthew's pioneering work into a fuller statement of Jesus' teachings.

CHAPTER 7

Quoting the Old Testament

1. OT quotations in The Sayings probably from the targums

There is a strong possibility that when the Apostle Matthew quoted the Old Testament in *The Sayings*, he didn't use the Masoretic Text (the standard Hebrew text of the Old Testament) or the Septuagint (the Greek translation of the Old Testament made in Alexandria between 275 BC and 150 BC). Instead, he used an Aramaic translation of the Old Testament, called a *targum*. The word *targum* means *translation* in Aramaic.

2. The origin of the targums

When the Jews returned from the Babylonian Captivity in 538 BC they no longer spoke Hebrew. They spoke Aramaic as their daily language and restricted the use of Hebrew to religious services and other formal activities. The Torah (Genesis through Deuteronomy) was probably translated into Aramaic by about 200 BC. Thus there was a *targum* of the Torah. Later most of the rest of the Old Testament was translated into Aramaic, but in sections rather than as one whole book (for example, there was a *targum* of Job, a *targum* of the Psalms, a *targum* of the Minor Prophets, etc). These Aramaic *targums* were often read in synagogue after the Hebrew readings, which the people didn't understand.

3. Why the targums have been overlooked

Ancient manuscripts were made of papyrus or leather and didn't last long, unless they were kept in a sealed container in a dry climate (such as Egypt). Otherwise, they had to be continuously re-copied. The reason why so much Greek and Roman and early Christian literature survives today is that the monks kept re-copying them throughout the Middle Ages (until the invention of printing about 1450).

Until recently, the oldest surviving *targums* were from the Middle Ages, about 900 AD or later, and scholars weren't sure whether they really went back to antiquity, or were written for the first time about 900 AD. Another problem with the *targums* is that often instead of always giving an exact translation, they often give a loose translation or a paraphrase. And occasionally, but not very often, they mix explanatory material or comments into the text.

MAJOR VERSIONS OF THE OLD TESTAMENT

There were four major versions of the Old Testament before the time of Jesus:

1) The traditional Hebrew text, later called the Masoretic Text, which according to tradition was written in stages between 1500 and 450 BC. This is the same as the Old Testament in the Protestant Bible, except that many of the books are in a different order. In Jesus' time it was often called "the Law and the Prophets."

2) The Samaritan text, written in the Samaritan dialect of Hebrew in the Old Hebrew alphabet, and which consists only of the Pentateuch (the Torah). It may have been written about 500 BC, or earlier. It differs from the regular Hebrew Torah mainly in that it declares the temple in the Samaritan capital Shechem to be the true Temple (not the Temple in Jerusalem).

3) The Septuagint (abbreviated LXX), a Greek translation of the Old Testament that is of uneven quality, and contains about a dozen extra books (which Protestants call the Apocrypha). It was used by the large Jewish community in Alexandria, Egypt, most of whom spoke Greek. Most of the books in the Septuagint were translated into Greek separately between 300 and 150 BC. The early Church generally used the Septuagint as its Old Testament, and the Catholics and Greek Orthodox still use it as their Old Testament. The origin of the Septuagint's extra books is incertain. It was long thought that the extra books weren't based on Hebrew originals, but Hebrew or Aramaic copies (or fragments) of almost all of the extra books have been found among the Dead Sea Scrolls.

4) The Targums are Aramaic translations of Old Testament books, or parts of the Old Testament (such as the Torah or the Psalms). The various targums cover the entire Old Testament. It was once thought that they were created in the Middle Ages, but it is now known that some (perhaps all) of them go back to the Second Temple period (540 BC - 70 AD). They were created because after about 500 BC many Jews spoke only Aramaic.

Christian scholars have therefore made little use of the *targums* in studying the Old Testament, or in studying the use of Old Testament material in the New Testament. This is unfortunate because the *targums* are often quoted in the New Testament, although this is not widely known. Instead, scholars have assigned all of the New Testament's Old Testament quotations to either the Masoretic text or to the Septuagint, when in fact many of them come from the *targums*.

4. Recent recognition of the targums' value

In recent years, however, the situation has been changing. In 1930 Paul Kahle, editor of the *Biblia Hebraica*, published fragments of *targums* and other writings found in the Cairo Genizah (the hidden room in the Old Cairo synagogue where worn-out copies of religious books were stored instead of being destroyed). The oldest *targum* fragments from the Cairo Geniza dated from about 600 AD. In the 1950s the *Codex Neofiti* was found in the Vatican library. It contains the complete Torah and was copied about 150 AD (or earlier according to some scholars). The Dead Sea Scrolls, found in 1947, contain fragments of a *targum* of Leviticus (4QtgLev) and two-thirds of a *targum* of Job (11QtgJob), both dating back to before 70 AD, when Qumran was destroyed by the Romans. It is thus possible that the *targums* copied in the Middle Ages preserve translations going back to antiquity.

5. Some targum readings that cast light on the NT

There are many places where the *targums* contain readings identical with (or very close to) an OT quotation in the NT, which is different from the reading found in the Masoretic Text or the Septuagint. For example, in Mark 4:12 Jesus paraphrases Isaiah 6:9-10, "...that seeing they may see and not perceive, and hearing they may hear and not understand, lest at any time they should be converted and their sins should be forgiven them." Only the *Isaiah Targum* says *forgive*: the Masoretic Text and the Septuagint both say *heal*. Jesus' wording of Isaiah 6:10 comes from a *targum* version that would have been read in a first-century synagogue.

For a second example, in Mark 9:47-48 Jesus warns His followers to be ware of being "cast into Gehenna, where their worm does not die, and the fire is not quenched."[26] This is a quotation from Isaiah 66:24, except that

---

26   The King James Bible uses the phrase *hell fire* here, but the Greek text of Mark says *Gehenna* in verses 43, 45, and 47, and most twentieth-century translations say *Gehenna* in those verses.

the Hebrew text of 66:24 doesn't mention *Gehenna*. But the *Isaiah Targum* does, "for their breaths will not die and their fire shall not be quenched, and the wicked shall be judged in Gehenna." Jesus' warning in verses 47-48 combines the Hebrew and *targum* readings of Isaiah 66:24.

6. "With the measure you measure..."

Next, Matthew 7:2 and Luke 6:38 (both in the Sermon of the Mount/Plain that we examined earlier) give a saying of Jesus, "with what measure ye mete, it shall be measured to you again." This is a quotation from *Isaiah Targum* 27:8, "with the measure with which you were measuring they will measure to you." The Hebrew text of Isaiah 27:8 as we have it today is obscure. It has either been garbled in the course of successive copyings, or contains words or expressions that we don't know. "Measure by measure" is a possible meaning of the first word; the rest of the sentence doesn't add up.

The King James Bible says, "in measure... thou wilt debate with it." Some modern translations interpret the first word as "warfare" or "expulsion," and then give conjectural constructions of the rest of the verse based on that. Among the Jewish translations, the Jewish Publication Society's 1917 version says "in full measure, when Thou sendest her away...," while the JPS's 1985 *Tanakh* gives "assailing them with fury unchained..." with a note stating that the verse's meaning is uncertain. Jesus quotes the *targum* version, which surely gives the verse's correct meaning because He chose to use it.

7. The Parable of the Wicked Vineyard Tenants

Next is the parable of the Wicked Vineyard Tenants, given in Mark 12:1-11 (and Matthew 21:33-40). This is based on the "Song of the Vineyard" in Isaiah 5:1-7. In the Hebrew text, the Beloved One (God) plants a vineyard with a tower and a wine-press. But the vineyard workers (the people of Israel) produced wild grapes instead of grapes. So the Owner will destroy the vineyard. In the Hebrew text, the "Song of the Vineyard" is directed against the people of Israel.

In the *Isaiah Targum*, God didn't build a *tower*, He built His *sanctuary* in the midst of the people. He didn't build a *wine-press*, He built them an *altar to atone for their sins*. The people didn't produce *wild-grapes* instead of *grapes*, they produced *evil deeds* instead of *good deeds*. Therefore God will *remove the Shekhina* (His Presence) and *destroy the sanctuaries* (the Jerusalem

Temple and the synagogues). The *Isaiah Targum*'s version of the "Song of the Vineyard" is directed against the Temple and the religious establishment.

Mark's parable of the Wicked Vineyard Tenants is a prediction of the Crucifixion. In the parable, the vineyard tenants (the religious leaders) beat and drove off the owner's messengers (God's prophets), and finally killed his son (Jesus). At the end of the parable (12:12), the Temple's chief-priests (from 11:27) "sought to lay hold on Him... for they knew that He had spoken the parable against them." Jesus changed the story's "villain" from the people of Israel to the Jewish religious leaders, just as the *Isaiah Targum* did. The *Isaiah Targum* re-wrote the "Song of the Vineyard" with a new message that was used in Jesus' prediction-parable.

8. "Be ye therefore merciful..."

There are quite a few others, but the last one we will look at is Luke 6:36 (in the Sermon on the Plain), where Jesus says, "Be ye therefore merciful, as your Father also is merciful." The closest verse to this in the Old Testament is Leviticus 19:2, "Speak unto all the congregation of the children of Israel, and say unto them, Ye shall be holy: for I the Lord your God am holy," which says *holy* instead of *merciful*. However, the paraphrase of Lev 19:2 in the *Jerusalem Targum*[27] says, "...and say to them: My people, children of Israel, as our Father is merciful in heaven, so shall you be merciful on earth." This was surely the source of Jesus' statement in Luke 6:36.

9. Conclusion

These examples show that both Jesus and *The Sayings* used the Aramaic *targums* to quote the Old Testament. Possibly much more than is obvious. The presence of a *targum* verse in the New Testament can only be detected when that *targum* verse differs from its counter-part in the Masoretic Text or the Septuagint. Since most of the material in the *targums* were good translations, it is usually not possible to tell whether an Old Testament quotation in one of the synoptic gospels was based on the Masoretic Text or on a *targum*. However, the fact that Jesus and His disciples spoke Aramaic makes it likely that most of the Old Testament quotations in the synoptic gospels originally came from the *targums*. And this also makes it likely that most (or all) of the Old Testament quotations in *The Sayings* (and in the synoptic gospels) came from the *targums*.[28]

---

27 Formerly called the *Pseudo-Jonathan Targum*.
28 The possibility of harmonization of quoted material with the Old Testament by later scribes is a separate issue.

CHAPTER 8

What The Sayings Said

1. Can The Sayings' lost text be reconstructed?

Up until now we have examined *The Sayings'* few surviving parts (four medium-long quotations and a few smaller pieces), but have not addressed the rest of *The Sayings'* contents: the part of the work's text that hasn't survived directly. Reconstructing the broad outlines of *The Sayings* is not an impossible task. But it requires the logical and resourceful use of relevant evidence.

2. Evidence in the synoptic gospels' overlapping texts

There are three types of evidence regarding *The Sayings'* lost text. The first involves the texts of the synoptic gospels. Since *The Sayings* served as the major literary source for the creation of the synoptic gospels, it is possible to deduce quite a bit about the work's lost material by examining the synoptics' textual composition. The synoptic gospels are closely inter-related and consist in large part of over-lapping material. (This material has, however, often been modified in accordance with each gospel's specific purposes.)

Let's look at how the synoptic gospels inter-relate. The first canonical gospel was that of Mark, whose major (human) sources were *The Sayings* and the oral traditions given by Peter. The second canonical gospel was that of Luke, whose major (human) sources were *The Sayings*, the Gospel of Mark, information given to Luke by fellow Christians (some of whom may have been eyewitnesses), and very likely other materials. The third canonical gospel was that of Matthew, whose major (human) sources include *The Sayings*, the Gospel of Mark, the Gospel of Luke, Old Testament quotations, information given to Matthew by fellow Christians, and possibly other materials.

3. Details about how the synoptic gospels overlap

The overlap (or non-overlap) of synoptic material can be categorized as follows: Material in Mark which is also used in Matthew and Luke is called the Triple Tradition and constitutes a large part of the synoptic body. (93% of Mark's material is used in either Matthew or Luke.) Markan material which is used in Matthew but not in Luke, sometimes called the minor Double Tradition, is also significant but smaller than the Triple Tradition.

There is also a small amount of Markan material used in Luke but not in Matthew (such as the story of the widow's two mites in Mark 12:41-44); a small amount of Markan material which is only found in Mark (such as the story of the blind man at Bethsaida in Mark 8:22-26); and a certain amount of Matthean material which is only found in Matthew (such as the story of the vineyard laborers in Matt. 20:1-16, and most of the material in Matthew's genealogy-nativity-and-infancy narrative).

In addition, there is a considerable body of material, about 235 verses, common to Matthew and Luke which doesn't derive from Mark. This is called the major Double Tradition and is also known as Q (to be discussed in a later chapter). There is also a large body of material unique to Luke, called Special Luke, which comprises about half of Luke and is of uncertain origin but doesn't come from *The Sayings*.

Finally, there is a certain amount of *Sayings*-derived material in Luke which is not common to the other two synoptics, but also isn't part of Special Luke (because it comes from *The Sayings*, not from the supposed Hebrew source). One example is Luke 3:23, which says that Jesus was about thirty years old when He began His ministry, and comes from *The Sayings'* opening section (given in *Panarion* 30.13). Another example is Luke 22:15 (discussed briefly in the next chapter) which is from the Last Supper. Until now this material, which should probably be called L, has been mis-identified as being part of Special Luke. The amount of L is uncertain.

4. Estimating the size of The Sayings

Let us now apply this overlap (and non-overlap) of synoptic material to estimating the size of *The Sayings*. It is likely that *The Sayings* provided the structural core for the Gospel of Mark, to which Mark added material that he had learned from Peter. It is difficult to estimate how much material came from each source, and we will tentatively assign equal amounts to each of them. Since Mark contains about 600 verses, perhaps 300 verses derive from *The Sayings*. This would mean that half of the Triple Tradition derives from *The Sayings*.

(Of course, much of the material in *The Sayings* would have also appeared in Peter's account of Jesus' ministry, since both Peter and Matthew were eyewitnesses to Jesus' ministry. It is likely that in his crafting of this material Mark used *The Sayings'* text as the written basis for his gospel account, to which he added supplementary and correcting material from Peter's oral account. We have seen this pattern in the creation of Mark's version of the Rich Young Ruler. Therefore when an incident in the Gospel of Mark was found in both *The Sayings* and in Peter's oral account, the present writer has attributed it to *The Sayings* because that was the written basis for Mark's text. It is difficult to estimate how much of the *Sayings* material in Mark also occurred in Peter's oral account, but it was certainly substantial.)

Likewise, half of the Matthew-Mark double tradition, which totals about 140 verses, probably derives from *The Sayings*, since all of that tradition comes from Mark. Half of this is about 70 verses. And most of the Matthew-Luke double tradition, erroneously called Q, likely comes from *The Sayings* (except for Matthean material which was taken from Special Luke, discernable by underlying Hebraisms). Since the Matthew-Luke tradition totals about 235 verses, we'll guess that 200 come from *The Sayings*.

Finally, there is a small amount of material common to Mark and Luke only, and each of the gospels contains a small amount of unique material, not shared with the other gospels (but not including Special Luke), some of which may have come from *The Sayings*, adding a small amount to the total. This puts the total number of verses in *The Sayings* at almost 600. (Since the Gospel of Matthew contains the Triple Tradition, the Matthew-Luke double tradition, and the Matthew-Mark double tradition, it is the gospel which contains the most *Sayings* material -- almost all of it.)

There may be, however, one more block of *Sayings* material. There is evidence that *The Sayings* contained a small amount of material that the later gospel-writers decided not to use. One example of this unacceptable material may be the story of "the woman taken in adultery" (John 7:53-8:11, discussed in a later chapter). That story was not originally part of the Gospel of John, but was added to the Old Latin versions of John about 150-200 AD. Papias states that a story very similar to this came from *The Sayings*. And there may have been other material that the gospel-writers rejected (discussed in the following chapter). The total amount of rejected material is unknown, but is likely to have been small.

The preceding figures indicate that *The Sayings* was about 600 verses long. This amounts to a large part, about a third, of the total body of synoptic material. But bear in mind that this estimate is based on the assumption that half of the Gospel of Mark was drawn from *The Sayings*. If the amount of *Sayings* material in Mark were larger or smaller, that would increase or diminish the estimate of synoptic material derived from *The Sayings*. Either way, *The Sayings* is still the major literary component of the synoptic gospels.

5. Evidence confirming The Sayings' size

The second piece of evidence regarding *The Sayings'* contents continues the preceding line of reasoning. The *Stichometry of Nicephorus*, written about 810 AD by the head of the Greek Orthodox Church, Patriarch Nicephorus Constantinopolitanus, gives the lengths of all the books of the Bible and of many of the rejected writings. (This is discussed in a later chapter.) The *Stichometry* states that the *Gospel according to the Hebrews*, a later name for *The Sayings*, was about 2,200 *stichoi* long. A *stichos* is a line of text in a scroll or codex.

Since the *Stichometry* also states that the Gospel of Mark contained about 2,000 *stichoi*, this means that *The Sayings* was about 10% longer than the Gospel of Mark, roughly 650 verses -- not far from the above estimate. If *The Sayings* comprised 55% of Mark the numbers would work out better, but would still only be approximate because the actual size of some of the smaller components is unknown, and the numbers given throughout the *Stichometry* are usually round rather than exact. In any event, this means that *The Sayings* was about the same length as any of the four canonical gospels, not substantially shorter.

6. Evidence from The Sayings' Aramaic substratum

Let us now turn to the third source of evidence regarding *The Sayings'* contents. Scholars say that an Aramaic substratum underlies most of the synoptic gospels. This substratum is often visible in the grammar and phraseology of the overlying Greek text. Since *The Sayings* was written in Aramaic, it is likely that *The Sayings* was that Aramaic substratum. This Aramaic substratum has been studied by many scholars, but not with respect to *The Sayings*. A survey of Aramaic-influenced expressions and grammatical constructions in the gospels (an even some instances of untranslated Aramaic text!) would identify many of the passages derived from *The Sayings*. This in turn would provide a good starting-point toward mapping out (and tentatively reconstructing) the text of *The Sayings*.

And let us note that Mark's record of Jesus' words on the cross (*Eloi, Eloi, lama sabachthani? --* meaning *My God, My God, why hast Thou forsaken Me?*) probably means that *The Sayings* contained the first account of the Crucifixion, which would have been the basis for the Crucifixion narratives in the synoptics. The possibility of reconstructing the approximate text of *The Sayings* is thrilling!

An Intriguing Problem

Many early Christian writers testify that the Eionites denied Jesus' divine nature and miraculous birth, and also used Matthew's *Sayings* as their only New Testament Scripture. Could *The Sayings* have contained no material that conflicted with their beliefs about Jesus? If so, was this because *The Sayings* didn't originally contain any such material, or because the Ebionites later removed it?

---

7. Matthew may have changed The Sayings' layout

Finally, there is the possibility that the layout of *The Sayings* changed halfway through the work. *The Sayings* probably began as a collection of Jesus' sayings and parables, and nothing else. At some point, the Apostle Matthew started telling the story of Jesus' travels and ministry. This likely proceeded as a (roughly) chronological narrative, with much dialogue, and included the Passion, Resurrection and post-Resurrection events. Matthew never integrated the *logia* into the narrative, in part because Jesus likely repeated many (or most) of His statements many times in different settings. In the work's final form, Matthew must have placed the narrative section before the *logia* section, since Epiphanius states that *The Sayings* opened with the ministry of John the Baptist.

Thus the first half of the finished work may have consisted of a chronological narration of Jesus' travels and ministry, while the second half was a (possibly unorganized) collection of His sayings. We may call these parts *Sayings* A (the narrative) and *Sayings* B (the *logia*). This would explain Mark's use of *The Sayings'* narrative sections for the framework of his gospel, and his non-use of most of its *logia*. And it would explain the way in which Luke and the Mattheist used the work's *logia*. But this is only an interesting possibility, with no support from early Christian testimony.

8. Summary

In summary, the contents of *The Sayings* is in line with the general synoptic tradition, and constitutes the largest part of that tradition. (The other major component of the tradition was the material that Mark learned from Peter, much of which passed into the Gospels of Luke and canonical Matthew. Special Luke does not belong to the general synoptic tradition.) *The Sayings* was about 650 verses long, and almost all of it is preserved in the Gospel of Matthew. The Aramaic substratum underlying a large part of the synoptic gospels is surely *The Sayings*, and a survey of this substratum would provide a good starting-point toward reconstructing the text of *The Sayings*.

* * * * * * * *

9. Four longest surviving quotations

For the reader's convenience, the four longest quotations from *The Sayings* found in early Christian literature are presented here in the order in which they likely occurred in *The Sayings*. Altogether they probably represent about 5% of *The Sayings'* text.

The first is *The Sayings'* opening section, quoted by Epiphanius in *Panarion* 30.13 in three or four large chunks that are out of order, except for the first one:

> A. It happened in the days of Herod, King of Judea, when the high-priest was Caiaphas, that there came a certain man, John by name, baptizing the baptism of conversion in the Jordan River. It is said concerning him that he was of the family of Aaron the Priest, the son of Zachariah and Elisabeth. And all went out unto him... [At this point Epiphanius says that he omits many things here, probably including segment B below, then continues]... The people having been baptized, Jesus came and was also baptized by John. And as He rose up from the water, the heavens opened and He saw the Holy Spirit in the form of a dove descending and coming toward [*or* entering into] Him, and *He heard* a voice from heaven saying "You are My beloved Son. I am well-pleased in You." And again, "Today I have begotten You." And immediately a great light shone

about that place. They say that when John saw it, he said to Him, "Who are you, Lord?" And again the voice from heaven *came* before him, *saying* "This is My beloved Son. I am well-pleased in Him." And then John fell down before Him *and* said, "I beseech you, Lord, to baptize me." But He resisted him, saying, "Let it be so, since it is necessary that all things be fulfilled."

B. And it happened that John was baptizing, and the Pharisees went out unto him and were baptized, and *also* all *the people of* Jerusalem. And John had a girdle of camel's hair and a leather belt around his waist. And they say that his food was wild honey, whose taste was that of manna, like cakes *made* with olive oil.

C. It happened that *there was* a certain man, Jesus by name, about thirty years *old*, who chose us. And He came to Capernaum *and* entered into the house of Simon, also called Peter, and opened His mouth and said, "When I went by the Sea of Tiberias I chose James and John, the sons of Zebedee, and Simon and Andrew and Thaddeus and Simon the Zealot and Judas the Iscariot and you, Matthew, *who were* sitting at *your* tax-office. I called and you followed Me. For I wish you to be twelve apostles, a testimony of Israel."

The second is the "love your enemies" passage found near the beginning of the *Didache*, which likely formed part of *The Sayings'* version of the Sermon on the Mount:

Now the teaching of these words is this: Bless those that curse you, and pray for your enemies, and fast for those that persecute you; for what merit is there if you love those that love you? Do not even the Gentiles do that? But love those that hate you, and you will have no enemy.

Abstain from physical and bodily cravings. If someone strikes you on your right cheek, turn the other to him too, and you will be perfect. If anyone forces you to go one mile, go two miles with him. If anyone takes away your coat, give him your shirt too. If anyone takes from you what is yours, do not demand it back, for you cannot.

Give to everyone that asks you, and do not demand
it back. For the Father wishes that from His Own gifts
should be given to all. Blessed is he who gives according
to the commandment, for he is innocent. Woe to him
who receives; for if a man receives because he is in need,
he will be innocent; but he who receives when he is not in
need will stand trial, as to why he received and for what,
and being put in prison he will be examined about what
he has done, and he will not come out of it until he pays
the last penny.

The third is the version of the Lord's Prayer given in the *Didache*,
which may also have been included in *The Sayings'* version of the Sermon
on the Mount:

Our Father in Heaven,
Your Name be revered,
Your Kingdom come,
Your will be done on earth as it is done in Heaven.
Give us today our bread for the day,
and forgive us our debt, as we forgive our debtors;
and do not subject us to temptation,
but save us from the Evil One;
for Yours is the power and the glory forever.

The fourth is the version of the story of the Rich Young Ruler given
by Origen in his commentary *On Matthew*:

"Another of the rich men," it says, "said to Him, Master,
what good must I do to live? He said to him: Man, do
the Law and the Prophets. He answered Him: I did. He
said to him: Go, sell all that you possess and divide it
among the poor and come, follow Me. But the rich man
began to scratch his head and it did not please him. And
the Lord said to him: Why do you say, I did the Law and
the Prophets? Since it is written in the Law: Love your
neighbor as yourself? and behold many of your brothers,
sons of Abraham, are covered with dung, dying from
hunger, and your house is filled with many good things,
and absolutely nothing goes out of it to them. And He
turned and said to Simon, His disciple sitting with Him,
and said to him: Simon, son of Jona, it is easier for a camel

to pass through the eye of a needle than for a rich man
into the kingdom of Heaven."

In addition to the preceding four passages, the *Didache* contains several shorter quotations from *The Sayings* (most of which are listed in chapter 2), and early church writers also give a number of questionable quotations (most of which are discussed in chapter 9).

CHAPTER 9

A Book With Many Names

1. The Sayings was known by many names

According to Papias, the Apostle Matthew called his gospel Λόγια τοῦ ἡμῶν Κυρίου, which translates into English as *The Sayings of Our Lord*. The original Aramaic must have been זרמד אלמ, which transliterates as *Melê de-Māran*. The early church fathers had several other names for it:

> the Gospel of [or according to] Matthew written in Hebrew (this is by far the most commonly used name)
>
> the Gospel of [or according to] the Hebrews
> the Gospel [or Hebrew gospel] used by the Hebrews
>
> the Gospel of [or according to] the Ebionites
> the Gospel [or Hebrew gospel] used by the Ebionites
>
> the Gospel of [or according to] the Egyptians[29]
> the Gospel [or Hebrew gospel] used by the Egyptians
>
> the Gospel of [or according to] the Nazoreans[30]
> the Gospel [or Hebrew gospel] used by the Nazoreans

2. The Nazorean version of The Sayings

The last set of names was used for the version of *The Sayings* used by the Nazoreans, a Jewish-Christian sect that believed that Jesus was born of Mary through the virgin birth, and held several other orthodox Christian beliefs about Jesus, but nevertheless adhered to Jewish practices. Their version of *The Sayings* contained the first two chapters of canonical Matthew (the genealogy and nativity) and some other material from canonical Matthew. The Nazoreans were second to the Ebionites in size, and also began in the first century.

---

29 Not to be confused with the Gnostic writing of the same name.
30 The exact phrase "Gospel of the Nazoreans" doesn't occur until the Middle Ages.

3. Later Ebionite modifications to The Sayings

JEWISH-CHRISTIAN SECTS

1) Ebionites. The first and main Jewish-Christian sect, which descended from the Jerusalem Church and was centered at Pella on the Jordan River. They believed that Jesus was a special prophet from God, but not the Son of God in a divine sense; that He was born to Joseph and Mary in the natural manner; and that it was necessary to fulfill the Mosaic Law (circumcision and the kosher food laws).

2) Nazoreans. A Jewish-Christian sect in Syria that believed that Jesus was born of Mary through the virgin birth, and held several other orthodox Christian beliefs about Jesus, but nevertheless adhered to Jewish practices. The Nazoreans were second to the Ebionites in size, and also began in the first century.

3) Cerinthians. A small group in Asia Minor founded late in the first century by Cerinthus, a religious fraud who capitalized on the Apostle John's teachings about the Millennial Kingdom by promising followers an imminent paradise featuring sexual promiscuity.

4) Merinthians. Little is known of this group, whose existence was questioned by some ancient authors.

5) Symmachians. A sub-group within the Ebionites, named after Symmachus, a high-ranking Ebionite who translated the Old Testament into good Greek about 200 AD, and wrote biblical commentaries that attacked the canonical Gospel of Matthew.

6) Elkesaites. An Ebionite split-off group in Mesopotamia, started about 200 AD or earlier. In addition to adhering to the Mosaic Law and rejecting Paul's writings, the Elkesaites held docetic views on the nature of Jesus (i.e. that His human nature and suffering were apparent rather than real) and stressed the redemptive nature of baptism. They used the *Book of Elkesai*, written about a hundred years before, as their major scripture and were therefore called Elkesaites.

The later Ebionites were vegetarians. Epiphanius of Salamis states that they "do not accept the entire Pentateuch of Moses but reject certain passages," and gives as examples their objections to eating meat and sacrificing animals (*Panarion* 30.18.7-8). In their version of *The Sayings* Jesus says "I have come to abolish sacrifices, and if you do not cease sacrifices, [God's] wrath will not cease from you" (*Pan.* 30.16.5). This isn't in any of the synoptic gospels and likely wasn't in *The Sayings*. Also in their version of *The Sayings* John the Baptist ate honey-cakes instead of locusts (*Pan.* 30.13.4-5), and at the Last Supper Jesus told His disciples "I earnestly desired *not* to eat *meat* with you this Passover" (*Pan.* 30.22.4-5), whose synoptic parallel is Luke 22:15. The words *not* and *meat* aren't present in Luke and surely weren't in the original version of *The Sayings*. These three verses on vegetarianism and against animal sacrifices were later alterations to *The Sayings*' text introduced to support the later Ebionites' sectarian practices.

4. Other Jewish-Christian groups that used The Sayings

In addition, there were several smaller Jewish-Christian groups, such as the Cerinthians, Merinthians (if this group really existed), Symmachians, and Elkesaites, some of which also made modifications to *The Sayings* to support their beliefs. The founders of these groups were charlatans who sought fame and financial gain. The earliest of these were the Cerinthinans, and there is a story (which is probably true because it comes from Polycarp, who knew John) that once, when John was in a public bath-house in Ephesus, he learned that Cerinthus had just entered the bath-house and he (John) immediately jumped up and left in order not to be under the same roof with the scoundrel.

5. Confusion with Hebrew version of canonical Matthew

Let us also note that canonical Matthew, the Gospel of John, and the Acts of the Apostles were later translated into Hebrew (meaning Aramaic) for use in converting Jews and Jewish Christians to Pauline Christianity; and that early Christian writers sometimes confused Matthew's Hebrew gospel with the Hebrew translation of canonical Matthew, as Jerome did in *On Famous Men*, section 3.

And it should be brought out that, whereas some scholars have warned against assuming that every patristic reference to a Hebrew gospel refers to the same work,[31] the fact is that the majority of early church writers refer to the Hebrew gospel as the work of Matthew -- and it is unlikely that there existed many Hebrew gospels all attributed to Matthew. Rather, there was one Hebrew gospel, acknowledged as the work of Matthew, of which there were several versions that were very similar (except that the Nazorean version contained the genealogy and nativity).

---

31 For example, see Ray Pritz, *Nazarene Jewish Christianity,* p. 85.

6. Possible questionable verses in *The Sayings*

The Sayings of Our Lord may have contained a few questionable or troublesome verses. Some of these may be an instance where Matthew (and possibly the other Apostles) didn't understand what Jesus was saying (the idea itself) at the time He said it, and likely further distorted it when trying to reconstruct it later. Others may be invented sayings that were added to *The Sayings* later for whatever reason. There were probably only a few such troublesome verses, and they likely caught the eye of early Christian writers specifically because they were so unusual. Here are the main ones:

In his *Commentary on John* (2.12), Origen states that the *Gospel according to the Hebrews* quotes Jesus as saying, "My mother the Holy Spirit took Me by one of My hairs and brought Me to the great hill, the Thabor" (meaning Mt. Tabor, about six miles south-east of Nazareth, the traditional site of the Transfiguration). In other places, it is quoted as "Just now, My mother the Holy Spirit...," implying that Jesus was magically transported, in a second's time, to a distant location. This doesn't sound like something Jesus would have said, or that Matthew would have put in *The Sayings*. It sounds more like something from one of the later infancy gospels that told stories about the boy Jesus making birds out of clay, that then flew away. It was likely invented by an individual or group with mystical tendencies. The fact that several early Christian writers gave this as a saying in Matthew's Hebrew gospel, probably doesn't mean that it was widely known and associated with *The Sayings*, but rather that those who repeated it were borrowing from each other.

Next, in *The Miscellanies* (2.9), Clement of Alexandria says that the *Gospel according to the Hebrews* quotes Jesus as saying, "He who is astonished will reign as king, and he who reigned as king will rest." In 5.14 he gives a fuller quotation that he does not attribute to the *Gospel according to the Hebrews*, "He who seeks will not rest before he finds, and he who finds will be astonished, and he who was astonished will reign as king, and he who reigned as king will rest." This saying is also found in the *Gospel of Thomas*, where Logion 2 reads, "Let one who seeks not stop seeking until one finds. When one finds, one will be troubled. When one is troubled, one will marvel and reign over all." This saying is Gnostic in concept and not something that Jesus would have said. It likely derives from pre-Christian Gnostic teachings (Jewish or Greek Gnosticism). How it got into *The Sayings* (if it did) is uncertain. It may have been added later, or may have been a mistake on the part of Matthew (or a mistake on the part of Clement of Alexandria).

Finally, in his *Commentary on Ephesians* (5.4), Jerome states that in "the Hebrew gospel" Jesus says to His disciples. "And never rejoice, unless you look at your brother in love." This is almost Christian (the big objection is, what about rejoicing in the Lord?) and may very well have been in *The Sayings*. Or did Jerome find it in the *Gospel of the Nazoreans?* which differed at some points from *The Sayings* and which Jerome sometimes confused with *The Sayings*.[32] If Matthew did put "and never rejoice..." in *The Sayings*, this may be another instance where he misunderstood or mis-remembered what Jesus said.

Early church writers also attribute a few other questionable statements to Matthew's Hebrew gospel. If the Apostle Matthew wrote any of the above material, he clearly didn't do so with the assistance of the Holy Spirit.

---

32   And related to this, note that in his *Commentary on Ezekiel* (18.5-9), Jerome states that "the *Gospel according to the Hebrews* which the Nazoreans use ranks distressing the spirit of your brother among the worst crimes."

CHAPTER 10

The Verdict of Three Centuries

Matthew's Hebrew gospel and the Jewish Christians who used it were not forgotten after the first century. They were spoken of by more than fifty ancient and early medieval writers. Here is what some of them said in the period from 150 to 450 AD:

1. PAPIAS, who flourished about 130 AD, was the bishop of Hierapolis in Phrygia (now in central Turkey). His work *The Interpretation of the Dominical Sayings*, which tells about Matthew's *Sayings of Our Lord*, is now lost, except for a few quotations in Eusebius's *Church History*. According to Irenaeus, who wrote about 175 AD, Papias as a young man had known the Apostle John in his old age. Papias was very influential in spreading teachings about the Millennium (the thousand-year reign of Christ) to second-century church leaders.

2. HEGESIPPUS was a Christian of Jewish origin who lived about 120-190 AD. He wrote a five-volume history of the early Church entitled *Hypomnemata* ("Memoirs") that was directed primarily against the Gnostics and Marcion, but also included much invaluable information about the first-century Church. The *Hypomnemata* is now lost, but Eusebius drew much material from it, including his account of the death of James the Just in 62 AD, and other events. Hegesippus's work contained many quotations, some found in Eusebius, from a certain *Gospel according to the Hebrews* written in Palestinian Aramaic.

3. JUSTIN MARTYR, born about 100 AD, was a Gentile Christian from Samaria who taught at Rome. He wrote the *Dialogue with Trypho*, which defends Christianity against Judaism, and the *First Apology* and *Second Apology*, appeals addressed to Emperor Antonius Pius to stop executing Christians simply for being Christians. He was martyred in 165 AD. Justin speaks of two types of Jewish Christians: one group whose teachings agree

with what we know about the Ebionites (although Justin doesn't use the word Ebionite), and a second group (who were probably the Nazoreans) that differs from orthodox Christianity only in that they adhere to the Jewish law.

4. IRENAEUS OF LYONS, born in Asia Minor about 125 AD, was a pupil of Bishop Polycarp of Smyrna (about 70-156 AD, himself a disciple of the Apostle John). Irenaeus went to France as a missionary about 150 AD, and was bishop of Lyons from about 170 AD onward. About 180 AD he wrote *Against Heresies*, a five-volume work that is directed primarily against Gnosticism, but also considers many other groups, including the Ebionites. (Irenaeus is the first writer to use the word "Ebionite.") He states in *Against Heresies* (1.26.2) that "those who are called Ebionites... use the Gospel according to Matthew only and repudiate the apostle Paul, saying that he was an apostate from the Law... They practice circumcision, and persevere in those customs which are according to the Law, and consistent with a Jewish way of life, and adore Jerusalem as if it were the house of God."

MORE ON THE EBIONITES

Among the Jewish Christians, the largest group was the Ebionites, which began in the first century. (Their name comes from the Hebrew word *ebion*, meaning *poor*). They descended from the Jerusalem Church, which in 66 AD relocated to Pella, on the Jordan River below the Sea of Galilee. The area around Pella remained the Ebionites' heartland for several centuries. Their early leaders were *desposynoi*, relatives of Jesus. The Ebionites adhered strictly to the Law of Moses, including circumcision and the kosher food laws. They believed that Jesus was a special prophet but not the Son of God, and that He was born to Joseph and Mary in the natural way. They used the Old Testament and Matthew's Hebrew gospel (*The Sayings of Our Lord*) as their only Scriptures, and rejected the writings of Paul. The mainstream Church at first regarded them as wayward fellow Christians, but later considered them heretics.

---

5. PANTAENUS, who died about 190 AD, was the head of the Catechetical School at Alexandria. About 180 AD an Indian delegation to Alexandria, Egypt was impressed by Pantaenus's learning and wisdom and asked Demetrius, the bishop of Alexandria, to send Pantaenus to India to discuss religious matters with Hindu philosophers. Soon afterward Demetrius sent Pantaenus to India "to preach Christ to the Brahmans and philosophers

there." In Kerala (in southern India) Pantaenus found copies of Matthew's gospel in Hebrew, whose existence seems to have surprised him. The local Christians told him that Matthew's Hebrew gospel had been brought there by the Apostle Bartholomew, who had traveled to India not long after the Apostle Thomas's mission there in the 50s. When Pantaenus returned to Alexandria, he brought a Hebrew copy of Matthew with him.

6. CLEMENT OF ALEXANDRIA, who lived about 150-220 AD, is often considered the first Christian scholar. Born in Athens, he converted to Christianity as a young man. Moving to Alexandria, he became a pupil of Pantaenus (and may have learned of Matthew's Hebrew gospel from him) and succeeded him as head of the Catechetical School about 190 AD. The leading Christian philosopher of his time, Clement's thought was marked by the use of allegory in interpreting Scripture (which he passed on to his pupil Origen, who in turn succeeded him as head of the Catechetical School). He was very learned and wrote extensively. His most important writings include *The Outlines* (now lost), *The Tutor*, *The Miscellanies*, and *Who is the Rich Man who Shall be Saved?* Clement left Alexandria during the persecution of Emperor Severus (202-203 AD) and his later life is obscure. He mentions the *Gospel according to the Hebrews* in *The Miscellanies* (2.9).

7. TERTULLIAN, who lived in North Africa about 160-240 AD, was the first major Christian writer to write in Latin. Raised a pagan, he was impressed by the courage of Christian martyrs and converted to Christianity about 197 AD. Upset with the lax worldliness of many clerics, he followed the ascetic Montanist movement for several years, about 210 AD. He was a prodigious writer (31 of his works survive) and coined the Latin word *trinitas* ("trinity"). He speaks in *De carne Christi* (14) of "...Ebion who declares that Jesus is merely a man and only of the seed of David, which means He is not the Son of God..."

8. HIPPOLYTUS OF ROME lived about 170-235 AD and may have been a pupil of Irenaeus. He was a priest at Rome who was opposed to the lax moral attitude and heretical views on Christ of the several popes from 220 to 235 AD. He was elected by his followers as a counter-pope during that period. Hippolytus was a very orthodox scholar and theologian. He wrote the *Apostolic Tradition*, a church-order that details the rites and liturgies in use at Rome about 225 AD, *Against All Heresies*, which dealt with 32 heresies, and the *Refutation of All Heresies*, which connected Christian

heresies with pagan philosophies. He died a martyr in 235AD and was later rehabilitated and declared a saint by the Catholic Church.

Hippolytus was dependent on Irenaeus for some of his basic information on the Ebionites, but had a better understanding than Irenaeus of the differences between the Ebionites, Cerinthians, and Carpocratians. He states in the *Refutation of All Heresies* (Prol. 7.33.1) that Cerinthus, the leader of a Jewish-Christian sect similar to the Ebionites, "supposed that Jesus was born not of a virgin, but of Joseph and Mary, a son similar to all other men, but he became more righteous and wiser."

9. ORIGEN (about 185-254 AD) was a very important Christian teacher and theologian at Alexandria, Egypt, and the leading scholar of his day. He wrote prolifically between 230 and 250 AD. His major works are the *Hexapla* (a multi-language edition of the Septuagint), *De Principiis* (a systematic exposition of Christian theology expressed in Greek philosophical concepts), and *Contra Celsum* (a defense of Christianity against pagan accusations). He was severely tortured during the persecution of Decius in 251 AD, and afterward died of his injuries.

Origen, who appears to have had first-hand information, writes at length about the Ebionites and other Jewish Christians, but we will only give two quotations. He states in *Contra Celsum* (5.61) that "there are the two types of Ebionites, some who confess that Jesus was born of a virgin (as we do), and others who deny this and say he was born like other people." The first group would have been the Nazoreans, and the second group the Ebionites. And in *De principiis* (4.3.8) he says that "the Ebionites... are so called because of their poverty of understanding, since *ebion* means *poor* among the Hebrews..."

10. EUSEBIUS OF CAESAREA, called "the father of church history," lived about 260-340 AD. A native of Palestine, Eusebius was a pupil of Pamphilus, the Bishop of Caesarea who established a large and important library of Christian literature at Caesarea, and helped him edit biblical manuscripts at the library. Eusebius came to regard Pamphilus as his spiritual father (and later called himself *Eusebius Pamphili*, meaning *Eusebius, Pamphilus's son*) and succeeded him as bishop of Caesarea about 315 AD. He was deeply involved in the Nicene Council (325 AD) that condemned Arianism (a form of unitarianism) and created the Nicene Creed, a strong statement of the Trinity.

His *Church History* (written in Greek but widely known by its Latin title, *Historia Ecclesiastica*), completed about 325 AD, is a comprehensive history of the Church up until that time. The *Church History* makes ample use of earlier Christian writings that are now lost (probably from Pamphilus's library), and is valuable for preserving parts of those works. From 325 AD on, Eusebius was a close associate of Emperor Constantine. His *Church History* was tailored to justify Constantine's religious policies (to unify Christianity and transform it into the state religion of the Roman Empire, and to replace early Christianity's commitment to pacifism with new teachings supporting "the just war").

Eusebius distinguishes two types of "Ebionites": one group which are the real Ebionites, and second group (presumably the Nazoreans) that admit the virgin birth, but adhere to the Mosaic law and deny Jesus' pre-existence as the Logos and Wisdom (God). He states in his *Church History* (3.27.1-4) regarding the real Ebionites, that "the ancients correctly called these men Ebionites, because they regarded Christ poorly and meanly. For they regarded Him an ordinary and common man, born of the union of a man and Mary, Who became righteous only because of His progress in virtue. They held that the observance of the Law was completely necessary... These men also thought it necessary to reject all the writings of the Apostle [Paul], whom they declared an apostate from the Law... and they only used the so-called *Gospel according to the Hebrews*."

11. EPHREM THE SYRIAN, who lived from 306 to 373 AD, was born in Nisibis (in northeastern Mesopotamia) and lived most of his life there serving as a deacon. He refused to be ordained as a bishop. In 363, after the Romans were defeated by the Parthians at Ctesiphon and ceded territory including Nisibis to the Parthians, Ephrem emigrated with many other Syrian Christians to Edessa (in northwestern Mesopotamia). He wrote numerous theological and biblical commentaries and annotated the *Diatessaron* (the harmony of the gospels in Syriac used by all Syrian Christians from 150 to 400 AD). His hymns, esteemed in Syriac-speaking lands for their mystical and poetic beauty, are used in the Syrian liturgy. Many of his poems contain graphic descriptions of heaven and hell. Most of these poems were translated into Latin in the Middle Ages, and helped inspire Dante's *Divine Comedy*. Ephrem is often considered the most important early Christian poet.

In a short appendix to his *Commentary on the Gospel* (i.e., Tatian's *Diatessaron*), Ephrem states that "Matthew wrote it [i.e. his gospel] in Hebrew, and afterwards it was translated into Greek."[33] This statement

---

33 Ephrem's *Commentary on the Gospel* survives only in Latin and Armenian translations. Because the appendix disconnects with the preceding text and the Armenian version has many additions, some scholars believe the appendix is not authentic.

was made as part of a brief discussion on the origins of the four canonical gospels (Matthew, Mark, Luke, and John). From this, it appears that Ephrem believed that the Apostle Matthew wrote the canonical Gospel of Matthew, and that he wrote it in Hebrew -- mis-understandings about *The Sayings* that were common at that time.

12. EPIPHANIUS OF SALAMIS lived from about 315 to 403 AD. Born in Palestine and educated in Egypt, Epiphanius returned to Palestine to found a monastery that was famous for its asceticism. In 367 he was elected bishop of Salamis in Cyprus. A noted opponent of heresies, Epiphanius opposed the teachings of Origen, who often dressed Christian teachings in the language of Greek philosophy. His major writing, *Panarion* ("The Medicine Chest"), addresses eighty heretical groups (both Christian heresies, Jewish sects, and Greek philosophical schools) and deals with the Ebionites at great length.

Epiphanius says in the *Anacephalaiosis* (II, 5.1)[34] regarding the Cerinthians (a Jewish-Christian group like the Ebionites) that "they use the Gospel according to Matthew, partially and not as a whole..." He states in *Panarion* (29.9.4) regarding the Nazoreans (a Jewish-Christian group), "they have the complete Gospel of Matthew in Hebrew. For as I wrote in the beginning, it is carefully preserved by them in Hebrew letters... but I do not know whether they have left out the genealogies from Abraham to Christ." He also says in *Panarion* (30.3.7) regarding three smaller Jewish-Christian groups (the Sampsaeans, Ossaeans, and Elkesaites), that "they also accept the Gospel according to Matthew. For they too only use this, like the Cerinthians and Merinthians. They call it the *Gospel according to the Hebrews*, which it can truly be called, since Matthew is the only one in the New Testament who proclaimed and preached the gospel in the Hebrew language and script."

He says a little further down in *Panarion* (30.13.2) regarding the Ebionite scriptures, "in the gospel which is called by them *according to Matthew* but which is incomplete, falsified and distorted, [and which] they call the *Hebrew Gospel*." Next, he says in *Panarion* (30.14.3) regarding the Gospel used by the Ebionites and other Jewish-Christian groups, "for they have removed the genealogies of Matthew and begin, as we said before, with the words: *It happened in the days of Herod the king of Judea, when*

---

34 The *Anacephalaiosis* (called the *Recapitulatio* in Latin) is a small epitome of *Panarion* which is appended to *Panarion* in many manuscripts. Many scholars believe that the *Anacephalaiosis,* which is a clumsily written work, was produced not by Epiphanius, but by a later writer.

the high priest was Caiaphas, that there came a certain man, John by name, who baptized the baptism of conversion in the Jordan River, and so forth." Again, he says in *Panarion* (30.15.3) regarding the Ebionites, "they also use some other books, the so-called *Travels of Peter* which were written by Clement..."

13. JOHN CHRYSOSTOM (c.347-407 AD), Patriarch of Constantinople, was called *Chrysostom*, "the golden-tongued," because of his eloquence. Born and educated at Antioch, he joined a monastery in 374 and four years later became a hermit. In 381 he retuned to Antioch and was ordained first as a deacon, then as a priest devoted to preaching. He was austere in his habits and very moral in his personal life.

After the anti-Imperial riots at Antioch in 387 he gave a series of sermons which converted most of Antioch's remaining pagans to Christianity. In the years around 390 he gave expository sermons on many books of the Bible. These sermons displayed his ability to combine the spiritual meaning of Scripture with its immediate practical application, and established his reputation as the greatest expositor of Scripture. Nevertheless, he opposed the allegorical interpretation of Scripture and stressed the literal sense.

Because of his fame as a preacher, he was appointed Patriarch of Constantinople in 397. Refusing the appointment, he was kidnapped and brought to Constantinople by imperial troops. Soon after taking office, he disposed of the rich furnishings and other costly items of the patriarchal residence in order to provide for local hospitals and the city's poor. His strong stance against immorality provoked the wrath of the Empress Eudoxia, who intrigued to have him deposed and exiled to Pontus. He died there in 407 from the extreme conditions which he was forced to endure.

In his *Homilies on Matthew*, among the expository sermons written about 390, he wrote in section 1.3 that "it is also said of Matthew, that when those of the Jews who believed approached him and asked him regarding what he had spoken in words, to produce those things in writing for them, he produced a gospel in the voice of the Hebrews." The believing Jews were the Jerusalem Church and the gospel was *The Sayings of Our Lord*.

14. JEROME (347-420 AD) is traditionally regarded as the most learned of the Latin Fathers. He spent several years as a hermit in the Syrian desert, about 380 AD, learning Hebrew from a converted Jew, and becoming a disciple of Gregory of Nazianzus, one of the three Cappadocian Fathers. During this time he visited the Nazoreans at Beroea and examined their

copy of a Hebrew gospel which they alleged to be the original Gospel of Matthew. Returning to Rome, he served as the secretary of Pope Damasus I from 382 to 385. Because there were so many Latin translations of the Bible and of such varying quality, Pope Damasus asked Jerome to make a new Latin translation for use as the Church's standard Bible. Jerome lived the rest of his life in Bethlehem and spent the next twenty years translating what became the Vulgate Bible.[35] Of his many other writings, the most well-known is *On Famous Men* (called *De viris illustribus* in Latin), a series of biographies of important Christians, written about 393 AD to counter pagan Roman pride in pagan culture.

Jerome states that he translated "Matthew's Hebrew gospel" into Greek. It is unfortunate that his translation has not survived. In *On Famous Men*, chapter 3, he says: "Matthew, also called Levi, an apostle who had formerly been a tax-collector, was the first one in Judea to compose a gospel of Christ in the Hebrew language and alphabet for the benefit of those of the circumcision who believed. Who afterward translated it into Greek is not sufficiently certain. The Hebrew itself has been kept until the present day in the library at Caesarea which Pamphilus the martyr very zealously collected. I have also had the opportunity to copy this scroll from the Nazoreans, who use it in Beroea, a city in Syria. It is to be noted that in this scroll, whenever the Evangelist (whether as himself or in the person of the Lord our Savior) quotes the testimonies of the old Scripture, he follows not the authority of the translators of the Septuagint, but that of the Hebrew text. These two prophecies are from those books: *Out of Egypt I have called My Son*, and *For He shall be called a Nazarene.*"

However, it is clear from the preceding quotation that what he translated was not *The Sayings* proper, since the two prophecies that he quotes both occur in the second chapter of canonical Matthew, which wasn't part of *The Sayings*. The work that Jerome translated was either a Hebrew version of canonical Matthew, or (more likely) a copy of *The Sayings* to which the first two chapters of canonical Matthew had been added.

15. PHILASTER OF BRESCIA (died about 395 AD) was the bishop of Brescia, a city in north Italy. He was a staunch opponent of Arianism, and before becoming bishop of Brescia had suffered persecution under earlier

---

35   Jerome didn't translate most of the deutero-canonical books (the texts of these were taken from the Old Latin versions) and parts of his Bible translation were revised by others in the Early Middle Ages. In addition, the Catholic Church issued official revisions of the Vulgate in 1589 (the Sistine edition), 1592 (the Clementine edition), and 1979 (the Nova Vulgata).

Arian bishops. About 380 or 385 he wrote *The Book of Assorted Heresies* (*Diversarum Haereseon Liber*), refuting 28 Jewish and 128 Christian heresies. Many of these weren't real heresies, just individuals or groups holding unorthodox opinions on matters such as the names of the days of the week and whether the positions of the stars are fixed. His main sources, for the real heresies, were the works of Epiphanius and Irenaeus, and possibly Hippolytus. His book treats the Ebionites and Nazoreans, but doesn't mention their religious literature. However, he states in section 36 that "Cerinthus accepts only the Gospel according to Matthew."

The preceding are the main early Christian writers who speak of Matthew's Hebrew gospel and the Jewish Christians who used it. They include many of the most important Church Fathers (Justin Martyr, Irenaeus, Clement of Alexandria, Tertullian, Origen, Ephrem the Syrian, Eusebius, John Chrysostom, and Jerome) and evidence the early Church's long-lasting (if somewhat inaccurate) memory of the first gospel.

After 400 AD, Matthew's Hebrew gospel is mentioned only a few times. Theodoret (about 393-460 AD), the bishop of Cyrrhus in Syria who played a major role at the Council of Ephesus in 431 AD, states that the Ebionites "only accept the Gospel according to the Hebrews." John of Damascus (about 655-750 AD) and Theodore Bar-Khonai (early ninth century) both state that the Ebionites "use the Gospel," without further qualification. Paschasius Radbertus (about 790-860 AD), the Abbot of Corbie whose *Commentary on Matthew* made careful use of early sources, states that the Nazoreans "invented a special gospel for themselves -- I don't know the author -- which is appropriately called that of the Nazoreans."

And finally, Nicephorus Callistus (about 1256-1335 AD), the Byzantine historian whose *Church History* provided valuable material in defense of images and relics (and which was translated into Latin in 1555 and used by the Catholic Church in the Counter-Reformation), states that the Ebionites "use only the Gospel according to the Hebrews."

CHAPTER 11

The Fourfold Gospel

By the second century the Church had developed a tradition that there were four gospels, and only four gospels. Justin Martyr, writing about 160 AD, quotes all four gospels (Matthew, Mark, Luke, and John) at various places in his works, the *Dialogue with Trypho* and the *First Apology*. About 170 AD, Justin's student Tatian, an Assyrian from Edessa, produced a harmony of the gospels (a work combining the four gospel accounts) in Syriac. This work, known by its Greek title, the *Diatessaron* (meaning "through the four"), remained the standard Syriac version of the gospels until about 400 AD.

Irenaeus, who was a disciple of Polycarp (who in turn had known the Apostle John), was the bishop of Lyons, France in the late second century. Irenaeus was one of the earliest church fathers to state that the number of gospels is fixed at four. About 180 AD, he wrote a five-volume work known as *Adversus Haereses* ("Against Heresies"), which was primarily directed against Gnosticism. In volume three he wrote:

> Matthew produced a gospel among the Hebrews in their dialect... Mark, Peter's disciple and translator, also handed down to us in writing the things that Peter preached. Luke, Paul's companion, also recorded in a book the gospel that had been preached by him [Paul]. John, the disciple of the Lord, later... published a gospel while he resided in Ephesus in Asia. (*Haer.* 3.1.1)

Irenaeus then went on to give reasons, in the form of examples from nature and Scripture, why there are four, and only four, gospels: the four points of the compass, the four winds, the four-faced cherubim in Ezekiel 1, the four living creatures in Rev 4:7, the fourfold activity of the Word of God, and God's four covenants with mankind (*Haer.* 3.11.8). Irenaeus argues that the four gospels are actually one God-given gospel, in fourfold form, which declares one God, the Creator of heaven and earth, and one Christ, the Son of God. The four are held together by the Holy Spirit.

Origen, the head of the Catechetical School in Alexandria, declared in his *Commentary on Matthew* about 245 AD that the four gospels "are the only gospels in the whole Church of God that are undisputed throughout the world."[36] The fourfold gospel was the first canon of Christian Scripture, the core of those writings that later became recognized as the New Testament. Although Origen, Irenaeus and others stated that Matthew wrote his gospel in the dialect of the Hebrews, the Church regarded canonical Matthew as the first part of the fourfold gospel.

---

36   Quoted in Eusebius, *Church History* (6.25.4).

CHAPTER 12

The New Testament Canon

1. Old Testament was the first Christian Scripture

The first-century Church used the Old Testament (both the Masoretic Text and the Septuagint) as its Scripture. Although the gospels were accepted as containing Jesus' message, those writings which we today call the New Testament did not receive recognition as Scripture at that time.

2. Early reverence for Paul's letters and other writings

The letters of Paul and several other apostles, and the *Didache*, were revered by the Church from the late first century onward. Early second-century writings by Clement of Rome, Ignatius of Antioch, Polycarp, Barnabas and several others, and the *Shepherd of Hermas* (from about 150 AD), were given similar regard. Questionable writings such as the *Acts of Paul* and *Peter's Revelation* were widely used in the second century, but were not considered Scripture. (*Peter's Revelation*, written perhaps 125 AD, contains a lengthy description of Hell based on Greco-Roman religious beliefs about afterlife tortures, which unfortunately shaped the Christian vision of the fate of the unsaved for many centuries.)

3. "Fourfold Gospel" begins the New Testament

The "Fourfold Gospel" (the four gospels considered as a single entity) was recognized as inspired Scripture by about 160 AD, in part through the efforts of Justin Martyr and Tatian. Irenaeus of Lyons, about 180 AD, was the first Christian writer to use the term "New Testament" (*Haer.* 4.9.1). He insisted that the New Testament was as sacred as the Old Testament.

4. First surviving canonical list

The first surviving canonical list is the Muratorian Canon (also called the Muratorian Fragment), which was written in the late second century and contains some comments on its contents. The Muratorian Canon's manuscript is missing its first and last pages, and begins with the Gospels of Luke and John. (We would love to know what it said about Matthew and Mark!) It then lists the Acts of the Apostles, and mentions that Acts omits Peter's death and Paul's visit to Spain.[37] Next, it lists all of Paul's epistles (except Hebrews, which may not have been written by him) and states that the two letters said to be from Paul to the Laodiceans and the Alexandrians are forgeries.[38]

Next, Jude and two of John's letters are said to be received (possibly all three, since 1 John is mentioned earlier). John's Revelation and *Peter's Revelation* are listed as received, but it is noted that some don't allow *Peter's Revelation* to be read in church. The Muratorian Canon breaks off with a reference to the *Shepherd of Hermas*, which is recommended for private reading but not for use in church. Not listed are Hebrews, James, and 1 and 2 Peter.

The Muratorian Canon is significant because it appears to be a church document rather than a list based on private opinion. Its guiding principle for determining canonicity appears to be apostolic authorship, except that those writings are excluded that claim apostolic origin but contain unacceptable teachings. (Note that there are those who attempt to date the Muratorian Canon to the fourth century, in order to deny that the New Testament was largely established by the end of the second century.)

5. Eusebius's evidence

About 300 AD, Bishop Eusebius of Caesarea wrote his *Church History* (the *Historia Ecclesiastica*), which is our major source for early Christian history.[39] In chapter three he discusses the New Testament canon. He lists all 27 books of our present New Testament as being received by most of the Church of that time, but notes that James, 2 Peter, 2 and 3 John, Jude, and John's Revelation were not received by some. (Jude was objectionable

---

37 There has been much speculation about Paul's visit to Spain and certain modern forgers have supplied the missing material.

38 It has been shown that the Epistle to the Laodiceans is a *pastiche* (patchwork) of phrases drawn from Paul's other writings.

39 Most of the *Historia Ecclesiastica* was written in the 290s, but the last three chapters (8-10) were added about 324-325 AD.

to some people because it quotes the *Book of Enoch*, and introduces the quotation with a phrase used when quoting Scripture!) He also lists some books as being spurious (*nothos*): the *Shepherd of Hermas*, the *Didache*, the *Epistle of Barnabas*, *Peter's Revelation*, the *Acts of Paul*, and the *Gospel to the Hebrews*. Finally, he lists heretical works such as the acts attributed to Andrew and John, and the gospels attributed to Peter, Thomas, and Matthias. (It is not clear whether the *Gospel to the Hebrews* or the *Gospel of Matthias* refer to Matthew's Hebrew gospel.) Although Eusebius's list was his own opinion, it reflects the general view of the Church at that time fairly well.

6. Contents of the Codex Sinaiticus

The Codex Sinaticus, a deluxe copy of the Bible in Greek made about 325-350 AD, was found in the library of St. Catherine's Monastery in the Sinai Desert between 1843 and 1859. Some scholars think it may have been one of the 50 deluxe Bibles that Constantine ordered to be made for placement in major churches. Although more than half of the Old Testament (the Septuagint) is missing, the New Testament is complete -- the same 27 books we recognize today, including Hebrews and John's Revelation. The *Epistle of Barnabas* and the *Shepherd of Hermas* are given after the New Testament. Although the relation of *Barnabas* and *The Shepherd* to the preceding 27 books is not clearly defined, their position at the end of the list (after John's Revelation) seems to indicate a lesser status. The text of *The Shepherd* is broken off, and it is uncertain whether it was followed by other writings.

7. Athanasius's Easter letter of 367 AD

Next is Athanasius. It was customary for bishops to deliver a festal letter to their congregations at Easter. In his festal letter of 367 AD, Athanasius, Patriarch of Alexandria, included a list of the books of the Old and New Testaments. Athanasius proclaimed this list because certain unscrupulous men were producing false writings and deceiving many people, and he wanted his flock to know which books were authentic. Athanasius's list is important because it is the first canonical list that is identical to the canon used by the Church today. The Old Testament list was based on the Septuagint, but separated the apocryphal books into a different group from the Hebrew Old Testament books. His New Testament list was identical with the New Testament we use today. After the New Testament list, Athanasius speaks of two other writings, the *Shepherd of Hermas* and the *Didache*, as "supplements" to the New Testament. He says that they are not inspired Scripture, but have been recommended "from the time of the Fathers" as useful reading for new converts.

Books excluded from the Bible?

It is sometimes said that dozens, even a hundred, books have been excluded from the Bible or from the New Testament. Books that were once in the Bible and that the early Church used as Scripture. As evidence, they cite the *Book of Jasher* mentioned in Joshua 10:13, and the roughly twenty books cited in Samuel, Kings, and Chronicles -- all lost today. Or the The *Shepherd of Hermas* and the *Epistle of Barnabas,* included in the Codex Sinaiticus but not in our Bible. Or the *Gospel of Thomas, Apocalypse of Paul,* and many others found in the sands of Egypt. A multitude of lost scriptures.

This is often attributed to the Nicene Council or to Emperor Constantine, who sought to re-make Christianity in a new direction. It is claimed that most of the excluded books were completely destroyed and that only their names survive today -- and for some not even that. The implication is that the real Bible is different from the Bible we have today, and that Jesus' real teachings were different from what modern Christianity puts forward as His teachings.

What is the truth? For the Old Testament candidates, the answer is simple. These were source documents used in compiling Kings, Chronicles, etc., but were not divinely inspired writings and were never considered as such by the Jews. For the New Testament claimants, it's a little bit more complicated, but not much. Works such as *1&2 Clement* and the *Epistle of Barnabas* were written by the Apostolic Fathers (that is, Christian leaders of the first few generations after the Apostles) and were used by the early Church but were ultimately considered non-canonical because the authors were not Apostles. In the second century some of these writings were close to being on a par with some New Testament writings.

But books such as the *Gospel of Thomas,* the *Apocalypse of Paul,* etc. were Gnostic writings that were used by Gnostic groups, but were never used by the Christian Church. They weren't used by the Church because Gnosticism doesn't proclaim Jesus Christ as God, and Gnostic teachings are very different from Christian teachings. These books weren't read in church, quoted by Christian authors, or included in collections of Christian writings. They weren't excluded from the New Testament because they were never in the New Testament. Claims that these books preserve Jesus' real teachings and were suppressed by the Church come primarily from the New Age movement -- which opposes Christianity and profits by the sale of New Age books revealing the "real" Jesus.

---

8. Later canonical lists

It should be remembered that Athanasius was not did not originate this canon; he was simply recording the books accepted by the Church at that time. Four years earlier (in 363 AD), the Council of Laodicea (near Antioch) put forth a canonical list that included all the books of the Bible, except John's Revelation. In 393 the Council of Hippo (now Bône, Algeria) ratified a canonical list identical with that of Athanasius. In 397 the Council of Carthage (in Tunisia) confirmed Athanasius's New Testament list. The Church was now agreed upon the contents of the New Testament.

9. Gospel of Matthew always listed first

Finally, let us note that throughout the process of creating the New Testament, the Gospel of Matthew (canonical Matthew) was always placed at the head of the New Testament. The early Church considered canonical Matthew to be the first gospel. This was a muddied memory of Matthew's *Sayings of Our Lord* as the first gospel.

CHAPTER 13

The End of the Ebionites

1. The Ebionites rejected Jesus' divinity -- and declined

The Ebionites rejected Jesus' divinity and believed He was a prophet born to Joseph and Mary (i.e., no virgin birth). They believed that Jesus was adopted by God when the Holy Spirit descended on Him at His baptism,[40] that the Holy Spirit guided Him in living a perfect life, and that the Holy Spirit departed from Him when He died on the cross. This belief is called Adoptionism. The Ebionites adhered to many commandments set forth in the Old Testament, including circumcision and observing the Sabbath. They rejected the New Testament and used only Matthew's Hebrew gospel. They shrank in numbers and by the third century lived primarily east of the Jordan River (in Nabatea, Iturea, and Moab), outside the geographical mainstream of Christian development.

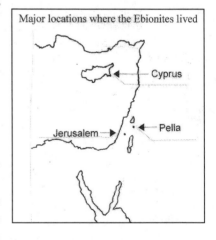

Major locations where the Ebionites lived

Philaster of Brescia, writing in the present tense in the late fourth century, says that the Essenes (meaning the Ebionites) "are those who exercise the life of monks, not eating delicious food, nor zealous for wearing fine clothing, nor owning anything. They live in secluded locations and devote themselves to study and good works. However, they do not await the Lord Christ as the Son of God. Nor do they recognize Him as the Lord announced in the Law and the Prophets, but they await Him as a prophet, believing that He is merely a righteous man."

---

40   In *The Sayings'* account of John's baptism of Jesus, after Jesus rises up out of the water the Holy Spirit *enters into* Him.

2. Jewish-Christians decline further

In the third and fourth centuries Church Fathers declared the Ebionites and Nazoreans to be heretical sects. Both groups continued to shrink in numbers. The Ebionites did not endure in the Transjordan, their traditional territory, much beyond 350 AD. According to Epiphanius, remnants of the Ebionite community -- possibly refugees -- were on Cyprus circa 375. Augustine of Hippo says in *Contra Faustum*, written between 395 and 400 AD, that the Nazoreans "exist until the present day or at least until very recently." Theodoret of Cyr says that by 450 the Ebionites were extinct in their other stronghold, Syria. The fate of the Cypriot community is uncertain.

3. Jewish-Christians disappear altogether

After the fifth century the Ebionites fade from history. It is uncertain whether they reconciled with Eastern Christianity (the Orthodox Church); joined the Karaites (a medieval Jewish group that rejected the Talmud as un-Biblical); converted to Islam; were absorbed by rabbinical Judaism; or simply died out.[41] The Ebionites were the continuation of the Jerusalem Church that moved to Pella in 66 AD and remained the center of Jewish Christianity for several centuries thereafter. In the end, however, that part of the Church that rejected Jesus' divinity vanished without a trace.

---

41 But note that Benjamin of Tudela and the medieval Muslim historians Abd al-Jabbar ibn Ahmad and Muhammad al-Shahrastani mention the existence of Jewish-Christian communities in northwestern Arabia in the eleventh and twelfth centuries that may have been Ebionites.

CHAPTER 14

Among the Heretical Writings

1. Background

After Emperor Constantine made Christianity the official religion of the Roman Empire about 320 AD, the Church held a series of ecumenical councils to resolve major theological disputes and to establish a uniform set of beliefs for all Christians. The first ecumenical council was the Nicene Council, held in 325 AD. The Nicene Council condemned Arianism (a form of Christianity that denied the Trinity) and created the Nicene Creed, which stated the Trinity clearly. Six more ecumenical councils were held in the next few centuries. The canon of Scripture was formally established between 350 and 400 AD. During the Early Middle Ages (400–900 AD) mainstream Christianity divided into two major churches (the Catholic Church in the West, and the Orthodox Church in the East), mainly for cultural and political reasons.

2. The Gelasian Decree

At this same time, both the Catholic Church and the Orthodox Church made lists of heretical groups and rejected writings. The first was issued by the head of the Catholic Church, Gelasius I, who served as pope from 492 to 496 AD. The split between the Catholic and Orthodox Churches began in 485. Pope Gelasius made reconciliation very difficult by claiming that supreme authority lay with the Roman see (based on Matt. 16:18, "thou art Peter, and upon this rock I will build My church..."), not collectively with the four other patriarchates (Jerusalem, Antioch, Alexandria, and Constantinople), and by doing this in a very high-handed manner.

In 494 AD Gelasius issued what is known as the Gelasian Decree, a catalogue of the authentic writings of the Church Fathers, which also included lists of apocryphal books and banned heretical works. (The Decree's full title is *Decretum de libris recipiendis et non recipiendis*, "the Decree on

Accepted Books and Books not Accepted.") Some scholars believe that additional material was added to the Decree about 520 AD. The Gelasian Decree is often considered the forerunner of the Index of Prohibited Books, which the Catholic Church issued between 1559 and 1948.

Section V of the decree (*Item notitia librorum apocryphorum*) contains a long list of rejected writings, 96 in all. Most of these truly were heretical writings, but some were orthodox writings from the early Church that were simply no longer used. One or two had once stood on the fringe of the New Testament, such the *Shepherd of Hermas* and the *Two Ways* (given in a re-worked version).[42] Also listed is a certain "*Historia* Eusebii Pamphili" -- this is, Eusebius's *Church History* -- which was included for politico-religious reasons. (See Appendix E, item 40.)

Index Librorum Prohibitorum

The *Index Librorum Prohibitorum* ("List of Prohibited Books") was established by the Catholic Church in 1559 as an instrument to oppose Protestantism. It was issued by the Sacred Congregation of the Index. Catholics were forbidden to read books in the *Index*. The 1559 edition listed about 1,000 books and authors, most notably Luther, Calvin, and Melancthon, and also covered works on astrology and the occult, and many vernacular translations of the Bible. After 1600 it included scientific works by Copernicus and Galileo that disputed the Church's position that the Earth was the center of the universe.

By 1800 the *Index* had about 4,000 entries, including most of the major figures of the Age of Reason and the Enlightenment: Descartes, Pascal, Spinoza, Kant, Francis Bacon, Hobbes, Locke, Hume, Diderot, Voltaire, and Rousseau. Copericus and Galileo were taken off the list in 1822. Nineteen-century writers on the list included Balzac, Stendahl, Dumas, Flaubert, Victor Hugo, Zola, and Anatole France. Twentieth-century writers included Sartre, Gide, and Simone de Beauvoir. In 1917 the Sacred Congregation of the Index was merged into the Holy Office (the new name for the Roman Inquisition). The last edition of the *Index*, the 20th, was issued in 1948, still containing about 4,000 entries. The *Index* was abolished in 1966, a few months after Vatican II ended, but Catholics are still supposed to avoid reading objectionable books.

---

42   The Decree also rejected the *Two Ways* in the previous section (4.5), in which it confirmed the rejection of all those writings which had been denounced by Jerome. In the first section of *De viris illustribus,* the section on Peter, Jerome denied the authenticity of a work ascribed to Peter, called *Judgment.* That work, *Iudicium Petri* (meaning *Judgment* written by Peter) was another name for the *Two Ways.*

The first item on the list is the *Travels of Peter* (*Itinerarium Apostoli Petri*, whose Greek title was *Periodoi Petrou*). It was used by the Ebionites, and was the main source document for the pseudo-Clementine *Homilies*. Item 6 on the list is given in some manuscripts as *Evangelium nomine Mathiae* ("the Gospel by the name of Mathias"), and in other manuscripts as *Evangelium nomine Matthaei* ("the Gospel by the name of Matthew"). This is probably *The Sayings of Our Lord*, which was now officially declared an apocryphal writing (*liber apocryphus*). That the *Evangelium nomine Mathiae/Matthaei* referred to Matthew rather than Mathias is shown by its high place in the list, near Peter, whereas a writing associated with the late and little-known Mathias would have been given a place near the bottom of the list.

Further down in Section V is a long list of individuals who taught various heresies and founded heretical groups. Among those listed are "Ebion" and "Cerinthus." At the end of this list, the decree declares these individuals and their followers to be "under anathemas, damned for eternity with an unbreakable chain" ("sub anathematis insolubili vinculo in aeturnum confitemur esse damnata"). This clearly states that the Ebionites and other Jewish Christians were considered heretics.

3. List of 60 Canonical Books

The second work listing rejected writings, the *List of 60 Canonical Books*, was probably produced in the seventh century (600-700 AD) in or near Antioch, then Greek Orthodox territory. After listing the Old and New Testaments, including books from the Septuagint, it lists 25 "apocryphal" works. These are the books of *Adam*, *Enoch*, *Lamech*, the *Patriarchs*, the *Prayer of Joseph*, *Eldad and Modad*, the *Testament of Moses*, the *Ascension of Moses*, the *Psalms of Solomon*, the *Apocalypse of Elijah*, the *Vision of Isaiah*, the *Apocalypse of Zephaniah*, the *Apocalypse of Zechariah*, the *Apocalypse of Ezra*, the *History of James*, the *Apocalypse of Peter*, the *Travels and Teachings of the Apostles*,[43] the *Epistle of Barnabas*, the *Acts of Paul*, the *Apocalypse of Paul*, the *Teachings of Clement*, the *Teachings of Ignatius*, the *Teachings of Polycarp*, the *Gospel according to Barnabas*, and the *Gospel according to Matthias*. The last-named is given as *Matthaeus* (Matthew) in some manuscripts, and probably refers to Matthew's Hebrew gospel. The exact words *Gospel according to Matthew* probably weren't used in order not to confuse it with the canonical "Gospel according to Matthew."

---

43   Probably two separate works, the *Didache* and the *Travels of Peter*.

4. Stichometry of Nicephorus

The third work listing rejected writings was the *Stichometry of Nicephorus*. It was produced during the iconoclastic controversy -- the bitter dispute over whether it was permissible to venerate icons (images of saints, etc.) that rocked the Greek Orthodox Church from 725 to 842 AD. The iconoclasts went around smashing icons in Greek Orthodox churches. Nicephorus Constantinopolis was the Patriarch of Constantinople (the head of the Greek Orthodox Church) from 806 to 815 AD. And he was the champion of the orthodox view (which supported the veneration of icons) during the second iconoclastic contest, which began in 814. He was removed from office when the iconoclasts temporarily gained the upper hand in 815.

The *Stichometry of Nicephorus* was produced by Nicephorus about 810 AD. Since Nicephorus was the head of the Greek Orthodox Church, his writing may be considered an official statement by the Orthodox Church. The *Stichometry* lists the books of the Bible and gives a line-count for each of them. (A *stichos* is a line of writing.) The *Stichometry* divides the Scriptural writings into four groups: the Old Testament, the New Testament, some Septuagint books, and four New Testament apocrypha (*antilegontai*). The New Testament apocrypha consist of the *Apocalypse of John*, the *Apocalypse of Peter*, the *Epistle of Barnabas*, and the *Gospel according to the Hebrews*. The last-named book is probably *The Sayings of Our Lord*.

Note that *The Stichometry* gives the length of the *Gospel according to the Hebrews* as 2200 *stichoi*. Since *The Stichometry* gives the lengths of all the books of the Bible, it may be possible to get from this an idea of how long *The Sayings of Our Lord* was. *The Stichometry* gives the length of the Gospel of Mark as 2000 *stichoi*; Matthew as 2500 *stichoi*; Luke as 2600 *stichoi*; and John as 2300 *stichoi*. This means that the *Gospel according to the Hebrews* (which probably means *The Sayings of Our Lord*) was longer than the Gospel of Mark but shorter than that of John. It was about the same length as any of the four canonical gospels, not substantially shorter than them.

5. The Sayings become forgotten and lost

There is little doubt that the three writings considered above are all *The Sayings of Our Lord*. The three preceding works -- the Gelasian Decree, the *List of 60 Canonical Books*, and the *Stichometry of Nicephorus* -- do not list books that were unknown till then, appear just one time, and then disappear. Rather, their lists are largely overlapping because the status of certain works as rejected writings was largely established. The *Gospel by the name of Matthew* (or *Matthias*), the *Gospel according to Matthew* (or *Matthias*), and the *Gospel according to the Hebrews* are three names for the same writing, a writing connected with the Apostle Matthew and with the Hebrew Christians, a writing which can only be *The Sayings of Our Lord*.

The Gelasian Decree, the *List of 60 Canonical Books*, and the *Stichometry of Nicephorus* contain the only surviving lists of rejected books from the Early Middle Ages. All three appear to include *The Sayings*. These lists show that by the Early Middle Ages, *The Sayings of Our Lord* -- the first gospel, written by the Apostle Matthew, and also the first Christian writing -- was considered a rejected writing. From 40 to 65 AD it had been highly valued as the Church's only written account of Jesus' ministry. By 500 AD it was considered a rejected writing, grouped with heretical works and forgeries. In the centuries that followed it was forgotten and almost lost.

CHAPTER 15

Why The Sayings was Forgotten

The Sayings of Our Lord was the first gospel (and the first Christian writing!) and played a key role in preserving memory of Jesus' words and deeds. But *The Sayings* itself eventually became forgotten, and its text lost. How did this happen?

1. The Sayings was used by the first Christians

The Sayings was used by the Jerusalem Church and must have played an important role in Christian religious services 40-75 AD, both in preaching to the congregation and as part of the liturgy. It was also surely used in proclaiming the gospel to fellow Jews and in showing how Jesus fulfilled Old Testament prophecies regarding the messiah. During this time *The Sayings* was translated into Greek for the benefit of Greek-speaking Jews, who were numerous in Antioch and Alexandria, and was no doubt used in those places both in religious services and in converting others to Jewish Christianity.

2. The canonical gospels appear after 65 AD

After about 50 AD, however, Paul began spreading the new faith into the Gentile world. He taught that Jesus was the Son of God, that He died for our sins, and that it was not necessary for Gentile converts to carry out non-essentials such as circumcision and the kosher food rules. Paul, who emphasized different parts of Jesus' teachings than those recorded in *The Sayings*, never quotes *The Sayings* in his epistles, although he often cites the Old Testament. Paul's Christian message had a different focus than that of many members of the Jerusalem Church.

After Paul's death in 62 AD, the canonical gospels began to appear, and the Acts of the Apostles. These were written in Greek and proclaimed

Paul's message about Christ, and were intended for Pauline Christians. The first of these, the Gospel of Mark from 65 AD, would have been rejected by many Jewish Christians because of its Pauline theology. Likewise for the Gospel of Luke and the Acts of the Apostles, both circa 70 AD. The new Gospel of Matthew, created about 75 AD, combined almost all of the old "gospel of Matthew" with Pauline teachings and proclamations of the fulfillment of prophecies regarding the messiah, and was quickly accepted as its replacement among the Pauline churches.

3. The canonical gospels replace The Sayings after 75 AD

In the following years, the new canonical gospels, especially the Gospel of Matthew, supplanted *The Sayings* in liturgy and preaching throughout the Pauline Christian world. (Although some of the *dominical sayings*, which likely came from *The Sayings of Our Lord* and are called *dominical sayings* for that reason, continued in liturgical use for some years. And it is possible that some of the Matthean citations in *1 Clement*, written about 95 AD, are actually from *The Sayings*.)

Only the remnant of the Jerusalem Church, which had moved to Pella in 66 AD, continued to use *The Sayings* as its gospel. It is unlikely that Pauline churches continued to make copies of the Greek versions of *The Sayings* after about 75 AD, and that worn-out copies of *The Sayings* weren't replaced after that time -- or rather, they were replaced with copies of the new Gospel of Matthew.

4. The mainstream Church forgets The Sayings

At first the mainstream Church must have remembered that the Apostle Matthew wrote the first gospel, the gospel that was expanded into the Gospel of Matthew. In time however, the use of the new Matthew became universal in the mainstream Church, and many either forgot Matthew's original gospel or thought it was essentially the same as canonical Matthew.

The new Gospel of Matthew's replacement of Matthew's *Sayings* was so complete that even Papias apparently thought something similar to this. His statement that many individuals translated Matthew's Hebrew gospel (which I will call "proto-Matthew") into Greek cannot mean that there were many Greek versions of canonical Matthew in the first century, for there surely were not -- there was only the one. He must be saying that there were many Greek translations of "proto-Matthew" in the first century. It therefore stands to reason that Papias didn't consider the differences between "proto-Matthew" and canonical Matthew to be significant; he felt that they were essentially the same work. The significance of the lack of the genealogy/nativity in "proto-Matthew" had not yet arisen at that time.

5. Growing gap between the Church and Jewish-Christians

In the course of the second and third centuries (100-300 AD), the gap between the mainstream Church and the (now small and isolated) Jewish-Christian community widened. Although Justin Martyr (c. 150 AD) may have considered the Ebionites as wayward Christian brothers, when Irenaeus of Lyons wrote about them in *Against Heresies* (about 175 AD), he zeroed in on some of their unorthodox beliefs. But Irenaeus spoke only of their repudiation of Paul and veneration of Jerusalem, not their rejection of Jesus' divinity.

At this same time (about 180 AD), Pantaenus, the head of the Catechetical School in Alexandria, found a copy of Matthew's Hebrew gospel in India and brought it back to Alexandria with him -- evidence that the work wasn't well-known in the western Church at that time. About 200 AD the Ebionite leader Symmachus was writing commentaries against canonical Matthew, and thirty or forty years after that Origen was writing pejoratively about the Ebionites and their version of Matthew.

6. Jewish-Christians become considered heretics

About 320 AD Emperor Constantine made mainstream Christianity the official religion of the Roman Empire. The new official Church had great authority and soon set about defining exactly what constituted orthodox Christianity. By the late fourth century, the Ebionites were clearly considered heretics. Epiphanius of Salamis, the major heresy-expert of the time, dealt with the Ebionites at great length in his magnum opus, *Panarion* (c. 378 AD). About ten years later Philaster of Brescia wrote his *Book of Assorted Heresies*, in which he described the Ebionites as heretics on account of their beliefs about Jesus. Jerome called the Ebionites heretics many times in his writings. Augustine referred to "the heresy of Ebion." And Ambrose of Milan wrote that "the Son of Man is against Ebion."

7. Learned men thought Matthew's Hebrew gospel was canonical Matthew

At this time many learned men thought that the relationship between Matthew's Hebrew gospel and canonical Matthew (written in Greek) was as follows: 1) the Apostle Matthew wrote the canonical Gospel of Matthew, but he wrote it Hebrew or Aramaic, and this writing was the first gospel; 2) early on an unknown person translated this work into Greek; and 3) the Hebrew original was subsequently altered by the Jewish Christians by omitting the genealogy/nativity and by making other changes (in order to justify their theological beliefs).

8. The role of the missing genealogy

This was the position of Epiphanius and Jerome; and John Chrysostom and Ephrem the Syrian had believed something similar. (Jerome also believed that the Nazoreans possessed Matthew's original gospel -- which he believed to be canonical Matthew in Hebrew -- because their Hebrew/Aramaic gospel contained the genealogy/nativity material. In fact, the Nazorean Matthew was a translation of canonical Matthew into Hebrew/Aramaic.) No one put forward the possiblity that the Hebrew gospel used by the Ebionites was the original gospel written by the Apostle Matthew.

The shift in understanding from the time of Papias lies in that Papias understood that "proto-Matthew" and canonical Matthew were works with somewhat different contents (Papias just didn't think the difference was significant), while later writers, in addition to having received no accurate tradition about the contents of "proto-Matthew" (and therefore thinking its contents were that same as those of canonical Matthew), understood the theological significance of the absence of the genealogy/nativity in "proto-Matthew." It signified heresy.

They could not imagine that an Apostle who had known Jesus could have written a gospel that lacked material about Jesus' divinity. On the contrary, such a gospel should overflow with proofs of Jesus' divinity, as the canonical Gospel of Matthew did. To them, the Ebionites' gospel was not a key writing from the Church's earliest days; it was a later corruption of no historical or theological value. It belonged in the heresy lists, not the history books. And it would soon be there.

9. *The range of Christian literature narrows*

There was another factor in the disappearance of *The Sayings*. In 1999 the present writer published an article about another Christian work written before the New Testament, a writing that also became forgotten. The *Two Ways*, a Jewish moral treatise created about 50 BC, was used by the Apostle Peter as a base-text for some of his sermons and was long remembered in connection with him. It was incorporated into the *Didache* and was quoted as Scripture by church writers for several centuries. A canonical list from about 410 AD even lists it as a "supplement" to the New Testament.

But in the fifth century the Church began suppressing heretical works and narrowed the range of orthodox Christian literature. Some of the books condemned by the Gelasian Decree, such as the *Shepherd of Hermas*, the *Two Ways*, and Eusebius's *Church History*, were orthodox works that didn't belong in the list. The reason for their condemnation is unclear. During the Early Middle Ages these types of writings disappeared. The Church made few or no copies of the condemned writings and most of them have completely disappeared except for their titles. (Eusebius's *Church History* is the major exception.) At the same time, the importance these writings once had in Church literature was also forgotten. They became lost writings.

10. *The Sayings disappears*

It was the same with *The Sayings*. The Church made no copies of *The Sayings* and its text disappeared with the Ebionites in the fifth century. As early as the second century, because it had been replaced by the canonical Gospel of Matthew, *The Sayings* was no longer remembered as the first gospel, but was thought of as a later alteration of the Gospel of Matthew. By 500 AD it had been declared a heretical work and the Jewish Christians that used it had disappeared. By the Early Middle Ages, *The Sayings of Our Lord*, which was both the first gospel and the first Christian writing, had vanished and was forgotten.

A Thousand Years Go By

CHAPTER 16

A Woman of Many Sins

1. Questions about "the woman taken in adultery"

There have long been questions about whether the story of "the woman taken in adultery", found in John 7:53-8:11, belongs in the Bible. The story of "the woman taken in adultery" goes like this:

> [53]And every man went unto his own house. [1]Jesus went unto the Mount of Olives. [2]And early in the morning He came again into the Temple, and all the people came unto Him. And He sat down, and taught them. [3]And the scribes and Pharisees brought unto Him a woman taken in adultery. And when they had set her in the midst, [4]they say unto Him, Master, this woman was taken in adultery, in the very act. [5]Now Moses in the Law commanded us, that such should be stoned. But what sayest Thou? [6]This they said, tempting Him, that they might have to accuse Him. But Jesus stooped down, and with His finger wrote on the ground, as though He heard them not. [7]So when they continued asking Him, He lifted up Himself, and said unto them, He that is without sin among you, let him first cast a stone at her. [8]And again He stooped down, and wrote on the ground. [9]And they which heard it, being convicted by their own conscience, went out one by one, beginning at the eldest, even unto the last. And Jesus was left alone, and the woman standing in the midst. [10]When Jesus had lifted up Himself, and saw none but the woman, He said unto her, Woman, where are those thine accusers? Hath no man condemned thee? [11]She said, No man, Lord. And Jesus said unto her: Neither do I condemn thee. Go, and sin no more.

When the Revised Standard Version came out in 1952 "the woman taken in adultery" was taken out of the text and placed in a footnote, along with a note explaining that there were questions about the story. There was so much adverse reaction from the public that the second edition of the RSV put "the woman taken in adultery" back in John 7:53 and left only the critical note in the footnotes. Almost all modern Bible versions do the same thing. In addition, almost all Biblical scholars today believe that the story of "the woman taken in adultery" was not in the Gospel of John when it was originally written. Why?

2. Overwhelming evidence

The manuscript evidence against it is overwhelming. It is absent from all three of the great uncial codices from the fourth century: the *Codex Sinaiticus*, *Codex Vaticanus*, and *Codex Alexandrinus*. These are the three very important manuscripts that British scholars used to revise the King James Bible back in the 1870s. It is absent from all of the earliest copies of the Greek New Testament, although it does appear in most of the later Koine manuscripts. Among the Coptic versions, it is absent from all the Sahidic and sub-Achmimic manuscripts, and from the oldest Bohairic manuscripts. It is absent from the Georgian and Gothic versions, although it is found in some of the later Armenian manuscripts.

The passage was also unknown to the earliest Church Fathers. No Eastern Fathers cite the passage before the tenth century. The first Greek commentator to discuss the passage is Euthymius Zigabenus in the twelfth century, and he states that accurate copies of the Gospel of John do not contain it. The earliest Western Fathers -- Irenaeus (about 175 AD), Tertullian (about 200 AD), and Cyprian (about 250 AD) -- make no reference to it.

3. "The Pericopa Adulterae starts to appear in the gospels

The passage does appear in some Old Latin manuscripts (Latin manuscripts from before the Vulgate Bible was created about 400 AD). And it was known to Ambrose (about 390 AD), Augustine (about 400 AD). and Jerome (about 400 AD). However, in many of the Old Latin manuscripts it is marked with asterisks or obeli indicating that there was uncertainty about its status. But it soon found its way into most of the Bible manuscripts of the Middle Ages. Although in early manuscripts it was found in different places in the gospels, it was eventually placed at

John 7:53-8:11 in connection with John 8:15, where Jesus says "I judge no man." Some scholars have noted that the passage's vocabulary and style (more noticeable in the Greek than in English translation) are much more similar to the synoptics than to John's Gospel.

Fast-forward one thousand years. It was in the Bible that Gutenberg printed in the 1450s: "adducunt autem scribae et pharisaei mulierem in adulterio deprehensam." It was in Erasmus's Greek New Testament. It was in Martin Luther's German Bible: "die Schriftgelehrten und Pharisäer brachten eine Frau zu ihm, im Ehebruch ergriffen." And in Tyndale's New Testament. And in the Geneva Bible. And in the King James Bible. And it had been in the Bible for centuries before that. And it stayed in the Bible for the next 500 years -- until the 20th century, when textual critics found evidence questioning its authenticity.

4. Where did "the woman taken in adultery" come from?

So where did it come from? A similar story is found in two important early Christian documents. In Book 7 of the Syriac *Didascalia Apostolorum*, written 200-250 AD,[44] bishops who are dealing with repentant sinners are advised to do "even as He did with her who had sinned, whom the elders had set before Him and then departed, leaving the judgment in His hands." That sounds very much like the story of "the woman taken in adultery." This same material appears in the *Apostolic Constitutions*, written in Greek, in Syria about 380 AD. In Book 2, chapter 24, bishops are instructed to deal with penitent sinners "as He did with that woman who had sinned, whom the elders stood before Him, and putting judgment in Him, departed. But the heart-knowing Lord asked her whether the elders had condemned her. And when she said *no*, He said to her, *Go, neither do I condemn you.*"

5. Eusebius said that Papias said...

And where did these accounts come from? There is an interesting possibility. Eusebius states in his *Church History* (3.39.17) that Papias "related another story of a woman accused of many sins in the presence of the Lord, which is contained in the Gospel according to the Hebrews." That means *The Sayings of Our Lord*. Papias had read *The Sayings*, since he was familiar with its contents and wrote a book on interpreting the "dominical sayings," sayings or anecdotes of Jesus that were recited or

---

44 Originally written in Greek, but surviving only in Syriac.

read in church as part of the service. Many of the dominical sayings probably came from *The Sayings of Our Lord*, since church services were being held at least thirty years before the canonical gospels were written. Perhaps the story of "the woman taken in adultery" was sometimes told in church at that time.

6. Why wasn't the story used in the synoptic gospels?

So it appears that the story of "the woman taken in adultery" was in *The Sayings of Our Lord*. Why wasn't it used by Mark, Luke, or the Mattheist? It is remarkable that all three of them omit it, especially the Mattheist, who tried to include as much of *The Sayings* as possible in his gospel. "The woman taken in adultery" was probably omitted from the synoptics because the earliest Christians (including the gospel writers) felt it condoned adultery. Adultery inflicts great pain on the wounded party and ruins a marriage.

The New Testament lists adultery as one of several sins which, if not repented, would exclude one from the Kingdom of God. 1 Cor 6:9-10 says "Know ye not that the unrighteous shall not inherit the kingdom of God? Be not deceived: neither fornicators, nor idolaters, nor adulterers... shall inherit the kingdom of God." And Gal 5:19-21 says, "Now the works of the flesh are manifest, which are these: adultery, fornication, uncleanness, lasciviousness... they which do such things shall not inherit the kingdom of God."

The Shepherd on adultery

The Shepherd discusses adultery in Mandate 4 (condensed translation by the present writer):

I asked the shepherd, "If a Christian man catches his wife in adultery and she won't repent and continues to be unfaithful, what should he do?" The shepherd answered, "He should put her out and live by himself, but not re-marry." Then I asked, "What if the expelled wife repents and wants to return to her husband, should he take her back?" "Yes," said the shepherd, "and if he won't, he commits a sin [against God] and a great offense against himself. But he shouldn't take her back if she strays and repents repeatedly. For Christians are only allowed to repent one time. This rule [on separation, repentance and reconciliation] applies to both husbands and wives."

The *Shepherd of Hermas,* which says that a husband is obligated to take back an adulterous wife if she repents, was criticized by many early Christians for that very reason. Tertullian called it "The Shepherd of the Adulterers" (*De pudicitia* 20). A story in which Jesus is lenient on adultery was unacceptable. (Although the unwillingness of many early Christians to forgive adultery could be justified legalistically by Matt 19:9, "whosoever putteth away his wife, except it be for fornication...," this conflicts with the spirit of Jesus' statement in Matt 19:8 that God allows divorce "because of the hardness of your hearts.")

7. How did the story of "the woman taken in adultery" get from *The Sayings* into early medieval Bibles?

How did the story of "the woman taken in adultery" get into our Bible? How did it get from *The Sayings* to the Gospel of John? For this, we need to discuss the Western Text of the New Testament. The Western Text is a text-type characterized by many textual variations from the accepted text of the New Testament. The Western Text's best representative is a manuscript called D (the *Codex Bezae* from about the sixth century), but the Western Text itself is much older. It has been shown that the Western Text rests upon a Greek text that was current in Ephesus in the early second century, and

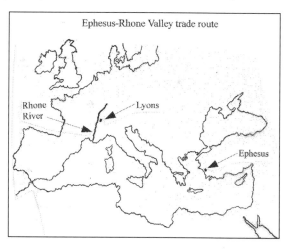

came to the Rhone Valley later in the second century, possibly through trade relations between Ephesus and the Rhone Valley. Irenaeus of Lyons went from the Ephesus area to the Rhone Valley about 150 AD. Did he bring a copy of that Greek text with him (even though he doesn't mention the adultress story in his writings)?

It then spread into some Old Latin texts, was widely found in Old Latin texts of the fourth century, and was later absorbed into the Vulgate. We saw earlier that another feature of the Western Text, the great light at Jesus' baptism, also came from *The Sayings*. It is probable that some of the stories and sayings of Jesus told by early Christians that aren't in the New Testament (what's called the *oral tradition*) actually came from *The Sayings*.

In short, the story of "the woman taken in adultery" wasn't part of the Gospel of John when it was written and probably comes from *The Sayings of Our Lord*.

CHAPTER 17

The Fragments

1. British-occupied Egypt and early archaeology

The *Description d'Égypt*, with its marvelous illustrations of Egyptian antiquities, published in Paris between 1809 and 1828, made Egypt an exotic place in the minds of many nineteenth-century Europeans. It was "the land of the pyramids." The gradual deciphering of hieroglyphic writing from the 1820s on furthered interest in Egyptian antiquities. The opening of the Suez Canal in 1871 greatly increased passenger and commercial shipping to Egypt and India. The British became involved in Egyptian affairs in the 1870s to stabilize the collapsing economy, and occupied the country as a British protectorate in 1882.

Construction of docks, harbors, railroads, telegraph lines and canals, begun under Ismail Pasha in the 1870s, increased under the British. The British also began Egyptian archeology in a serious way. Flinders Petrie, "the father of scientific archeology," started excavations at the Great Pyramid in 1880. Royal mummies found at Deir el-Bahri in 1881 received much publicity. And Grenfell and Hunt found countless papyrus fragments at Oxyrhynchus in the 1890s, including a sheet containing what appeared to be "lost sayings" of Jesus.[45]

2. Tourism at Thebes-Luxor in the 1890s

The 1890s saw a rush of tourism. The Thomas Cook travel agency, based in London, set up offices in Cairo and Alexandria to provide transport and

---

45 The mystery was solved in 1946 with the discovery of a collection of Gnostic writings at Nag Hammadi. The Oxyrhynchus papyrus was part of the first page of the *Gospel of Thomas*. Other important manuscript discoveries in Egypt at this time include the Nash Papyrus (two short texts from Deuteronomy written about 150 BC, then the oldest-known biblical writing, found in 1902), and the Codex W (a copy of the four gospels from about 400 AD, found in 1906).

lodgings for British and European tourists. The Cairo area had picturesque mosques and bazaars and nearby were the Great Pyramid and the Sphinx.

To the south, below the great bend of the Nile, were Thebes and Luxor, where the Great Temple of Karnak, the Avenue of Obelisks, and the Colossi of Memnon were located. Behind the many temples of western Thebes lay the Valley of the Kings. The Thebes-Luxor area was the number-one destination of most tourists.

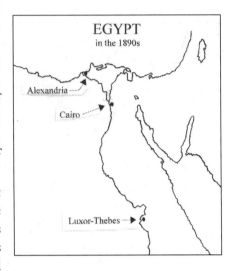

Perhaps the finest establishment at Luxor and Thebes was the Luxor Hotel. Built by the Thomas Cook firm, it provided first-class accommodations to travelers and tourists. Many were affluent people who sought to spend the winter season, when there was often snow in London, on the sunny Nile. From 1890 to 1901 the Anglican chaplain at the Luxor Hotel during the winter seasons was the Rev. Charles Huleatt. In the 1880s he attended Oxford University, where he had read classics at Magdalen College.

3. Rev. Huleatt acquires papyri that go to Oxford

Like Cairo and Alexandria and other tourist centers, Luxor and Thebes had many antique shops which illegally sold ancient artifacts and modern forgeries. There was a brisk trade in mummies, statuettes, old necklaces, and papyrus scrolls. And much grave-robbing to supply the demand. Some time in the 1890s Rev. Huleatt acquired three small pieces of papyrus with ancient writing. Perhaps he bought them in an antique shop. Perhaps they were a gift from a guest at the hotel. For whatever reason, the chaplain understood that they were valuable.

When he was transferred to his next post (in Messina, Sicily) in 1901, Rev. Huleatt mailed the papyrus fragments to his mother in England, with instructions to have them sent to Magdalen College. Rev. Huleatt died in the 1908 Messina earthquake. At Magdalen, Arthur Hunt (Grenfell's colleague at Oxyrhynchus) dated the fragments to the fourth century. They were then put in a display-case and ignored for a half-century.

4. *The Magdalen Papyri are re-examined*

In 1953 British papyrologist Colin Roberts re-examined the fragments and re-dated them to the late second century. They were then put back in the display-case for another forty years. In 1962 Roberts identified two papyrus fragments in the possession of the Fundación San Lucas Evangelista in Barcelona, Spain as being from the same codex as the Magdalen fragments, and dated all five to the second century. In June 1995 the Magdalen fragments were taken to Germany to be examined by Carsten Thiede and Gregor Masuch, who had invented a new type of microscope, the epifluorescent confocal laser scanning microscope.

5. *Description of the Magdalen Papyri*

The Magdalen fragments are small, about the size of large postage stamps. All three contain writing in ancient Greek on both sides. The fragments came from a codex, since codex pages are written on both sides, while a scroll is only written on one side. Each side contains several words, written in small capitals with no spaces between words. The problem is that the edges are torn, and many of the letters at the edge can't be read well because of dirt and spots. The new microscope made it possible to read letters that had previously been illegible and to make a better reconstruction of the text.

The codex was apparently a copy of the Gospel of Matthew -- all six sides contain small bits of Matthew 26 -- but the wording isn't identical with the text we have today. For example, the papyri's version of Matthew 26:31 contains the Greek word meaning "of you, " which is absent in our version of Matthew 26:31. And in Matthew 26:22 our text reads "and they were exceeding sorrowful, and began every one of them to say unto Him..." implying (in the Greek) that each of the disciples spoke in turn. The Magdalen fragment, however, reads "and very saddened, each of them said..." implying (in the Greek) that they spoke together. Since the three fragments contain altogether only about twenty words, two instances of different wording is quite unusual. If the fragments are representative of the rest of the codex, it would mean that the full text was considerably different from what we have today.

There are two other significant points. First, the name *Jesus* and the word *Lord* (referring to Jesus) are given *nomina sacra* forms (special abbreviations) reserved for God. This means that Jesus was considered divine in this text. And second, although the fragments match parts of Matthew 26, almost all of the text is dialogue, more characteristic of a "sayings gospel" than of the narrative-plus-dialogue found in the Gospels. It is possible that by some accident almost all the surviving text is dialogue, but statistically that's not likely. Again, it's very likely that the full text was considerably different from the Gospel of Matthew that we have today.

6. Re-dating the Magdalen Papyri

Drs. Thiede and Masuch were very diligent in dating the Magdalen fragments. In 1901, when Hunt dated the fragments to the fourth century, it was thought that the codex didn't exist in the first century. Today we know it did, and probably even existed in the first century BC. When Colins dated the fragments in 1953, techniques for dating based on handwriting weren't well developed. (The Magdalen fragments are too small for radio-carbon dating.)

Forty years later they were very accurate. One of the new methods involves finding a text of known date

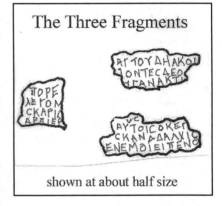

The Three Fragments

shown at about half size

that is an exact (or near-exact) match to the first text. The results showed that the Magdalen fragments were written in (or very near to) 66 AD, with a plus-or-minus factor indicating a possibly even earlier date by a few years, but not a later date. (A flaw with this dating method is that it assumes that everyone's handwriting changes gradually and uniformly in sync with the general change in handwriting -- which doesn't always happen.)

7. Discovery of oldest fragments of Matthew announced

This startling discovery was published in *The London Times* on Christmas Eve, 1995. It was soon broadcast in the media around the world. Thiede and British journalist Matthew d'Ancona published *Eyewitness to Jesus* in early 1996 (later re-issued as *The Jesus Papyrus*), and a documentary film soon followed. Thiede and Masuch were hailed as having proven that the Gospel of Matthew was written about 60-65 AD. And Bible scholars were left to ponder on something that couldn't be.

8. Canonical Matthew -- or The Sayings of Our Lord?

But there's more to the story. Some significant facts regarding the Magdalen fragments point in a different direction. First, although the codex appears to be a copy of the Gospel of Matthew, its text was different in places from what we have today. Second, the fact that the fragments consist almost entirely of dialogue may mean that the codex was a type of *sayings gospel*. And third, the date that Thiede and Masuch proved for the fragments (66 AD or earlier) is too early for the canonical Gospel of Matthew. Conclusion: the codex was a copy of one of the amateur Greek translations of *The Sayings*. The presence in the fragments of *nomina sacra* regarding Jesus means that Paul's teachings on Jesus' divinity were becoming widely known by about 60 AD, and were being applied to *The Sayings*.

And finally, although grave-robbing in old Egyptian tombs and cemeteries was reaching new heights in the decades after 1890, it is unlikely that a treasure as great as this was found accidentally in a common grave. Or that it was necessarily found close to Luxor. The likelihood is quite high that this invaluable codex was stolen from the antiquities niche of a Coptic church -- anywhere in Egypt -- and brought to Luxor because that was the best place to sell it. It was then broken up into a thousand pieces in order to have a thousand sales. What a pity! The loss of such a treasure!

CHAPTER 18

Possible Locations

1. Does a copy of The Sayings still exist?

Has *The Sayings* survived? Johannes Drusius (1550-1616), a Flemish orientalist and biblical scholar who had studied the Talmud and rabbinical literature, stated that copies of the *Gospel of the Nazarenes* existed in his time. Maximilian van der Sandt (1576-1656),[46] a Dutch Jesuit scholar of esoteric mysticism, also claimed to have seen the *Gospel of the Nazarenes*. The *Gospel of the Nazoreans* was a version of *The Sayings* to which had been added the genealogy and nativity and certain other material from canonical Matthew. Could a copy of *The Sayings* or the *Gospel of the Nazoreans* still exist today? Where might a copy be?

2. Is there a copy in Syria-Palestine?

First, under proper conditions ancient manuscripts do survive. The Dead Sea Scrolls survived because they were hidden in caves in a desert region, and those that were in the best condition were the half-dozen that were stored in a large pottery jar. Likewise, the Gnostic writings found at Nag Hammadi in central Egypt survived because they were sealed in a large jar. It is possible that archeologists one day may discover a copy of *The Sayings* at Pella, Beroea, or Kokaba (Ebionite and Nazorean centers), or on Cyprus (the last location of the Ebionites), or perhaps at Jerusalem, Damascus, Antioch, or Edessa.

3. In southern Iraq?

Second, there is the possibility that a copy came into the possession of the Mandeans, a quasi-Jewish, quasi-Christian sect in southern Iraq which claims descent from John the Baptist. They have a large, ancient literature with many

---

46   Latinized as Sandaeus, and also given as Sandäus (both without *van der*).

writings that are not all compatible with each other, and would not be expected to be in the same collection. Their literature has been studied, but probably not searched for an off-beat copy of the Gospel of Matthew.

4. A source for the Shem-Tov Hebrew Matthew?

Third, there exists a very unusual Hebrew version of the Gospel of Matthew, called the Shem-Tov Hebrew Matthew, which dates from the Middle Ages (or earlier). Scholars believe that the Shem-Tov Matthew was written in Hebrew because its vocabulary includes rabbinic language and Aramaic phrases, and it has many puns that work in Hebrew but not in Latin or Greek. It also has many unique readings that don't occur in any other manuscript of the Gospel of Matthew. Some of its passages seem to match passages in the Old Syriac versions, the *Diatessaron*, and the Gospel of Thomas. The Shem-Tov gospel is not *The Sayings of Our Lord*, but it should be studied to determine whether *The Sayings* was one of the sources used to create it. If so, the Shem-Tov gospel may shed important light on the contents and structure of *The Sayings*.

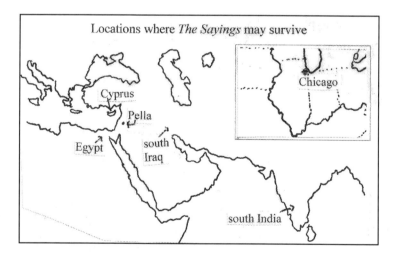

Locations where *The Sayings* may survive

5. Is there a copy of The Sayings in Chicago?

Fourth, as an Aramaic writing, it is possible that a copy may have been preserved among the Syriac writings of the Syrian Orthodox Church. The foremost expert on the literature of the Syrian Orthodox Church was Dr. Arthur Vööbus, who came from Estonia to America in 1940 and taught at the Lutheran School of Theology at Chicago. In the 1960s, Dr. Vööbus made trips every summer to the Syrian Orthodox churches and monasteries in Iraq (and occasionally to sites in neighboring Syria and Turkey) and was permitted by those churches and monasteries to photograph countless thousands of old Syriac manuscripts in their possession (most of which were later destroyed by Saddam Hussein). Dr. Vööbus died in 1988, and his large photograph collection is now housed at the Institute for Syriac Manuscript Studies at JKM Library, McCormick Theological Seminary, Chicago. It, too, needs to be searched for an off-beat copy of the Gospel of Matthew.

It is highly relevant that Dr. Vööbus admitted in his writings that among his objectives in photographing and examining those old Syriac manuscripts was the hope of finding an early copy of the *Didache* or a similar document from the Church's earliest years. He said that such a discovery would be the "motherlode" of early Christian research. However, there is no indication in his writings that he was aware of the document that Papias wrote about -- and which might therefore lie unrecogized among the many thousands of photographs that he left behind.

6. In southern India?

Fifth, there is the distinct possibility that *The Sayings* is (or was) preserved by the St. Thomas Christians of southwest India. The south Indian church was founded by the Apostle Thomas about 51 AD, a time when the infant Church still used *The Sayings*, and Pantaenus even brought back a copy from India to Alexandria about 180 AD. In the fifth century, Persian Nestorians revitalized the south Indian church, which for centuries thereafter maintained a large religious literature, mainly in Syriac. After the Portuguese arrived in south India in 1498, however, they soon gained control over much of the south Indian church and purposely destroyed a large amount of the old manuscripts (because many of them were Nestorian writings). What a shame! Nevertheless, it is possible that a copy of *The Sayings* escaped the Portuguese and is preserved as a relic in some south Indian church, or survives in a large collection of religious literature such as that of the Konat family in Pampakuda, in Kerala state.

7. Another copy in Egypt?

And sixth, it is still possible that another copy of *The Sayings* survives as a relic in another Coptic church somewhere in Egypt. It happened once before.

CHAPTER 19

The Inspired Word of God?

1. Should *The Sayings* be in the New Testament?

The Sayings of Our Lord was written by the Apostle Matthew, who had known Jesus and was specially chosen by Him to be one of His disciples and to accompany Him on His ministry. Jesus walked up to a man who could write and told him to become one of His disciples. He must have known that Matthew would one day write an account of His ministry, and probably chose him specifically for that task. The question therefore arises: Is *The Sayings* inspired Scripture? On the same level as the four canonical gospels? Pre-ordained by God to be the first gospel? A writing that should be in the Bible?

The Criteria for New Testament Scripture

The main criteria used by the early Church to determine whether a writing was Holy Writ (i.e. part of the New Testament) were the following:
1) *Apostolicity* -- whether it was indisputably written by an apostle.
2) *Inspiration* -- that its contents were inspired by the Holy Spirit.
3) *Orthodoxy* -- whether its teachings were completely in line with the historic teachings of the Church.
4) *Usage* -- that it had been used by the Church for a long time.

---

2. What is inspired Scripture?

In order to address these questions, we must first consider what constitutes inspired Scripture and how inspired Scripture is created. First, the Scriptures are both the words of men and the words of God. But they were not blindly dictated to their human authors by God. They are the product of both human authors using their natural gifts, and the guidance of the Holy Spirit, working in a way that ensures that God achieves His pre-determined purposes. The Bible is the Word of God in writing.

Second, 2 Timothy 3:15-16 says, "All Scripture is given by inspiration of God, and is profitable for doctrine, for reproof, for correction, for instruction in righteousness: that the man of God may be perfect, thoroughly furnished unto all good works." This says that if a writing is inspired by God, it will be profitable for doctrine, reproof, correction, and instruction in righteousness. Romans 10:17 says that "faith cometh by hearing, and hearing by the Word of God." Scripture that presents God's message to men is a basic part of God's plan of salvation.

3. How The Sayings measures up

This study has brought out several key points that bear on whether or not *The Sayings* is inspired Scripture. First, it has shown that the Apostle Matthew's collection of Jesus' sayings and doings does not adequately present Jesus' message and teachings. This is shown in the story of the Rich Young Ruler, where the Apostle Matthew related the encounter between Jesus and the rich young man without bringing out the full message that Jesus intended. *The Sayings'* account was based on the memory of the Apostle Matthew, who did not fully understand Jesus' message, and was written without the guidance of the Holy Spirit.

Second, the canonical gospels *do* present Jesus' teachings. In the story of the Rich Young Ruler, the Gospels of Mark and Matthew proclaim Jesus' commands to "take up the cross" and follow Him, and to "love your neighbor as yourself." These are key teachings of Jesus and they are placed in the story of the Rich Young Ruler in order to help instruct the reader on how to become a "man of God... thoroughly furnished unto all good works." Mark and the Mattheist wrote with understanding of Jesus' message, and with the guidance of the Holy Spirit, and their gospels are therefore inspired Scripture.

Third, the Apostle Paul played a vital role in revealing who Jesus Christ is, and the purpose of His death on the cross. The full meaning of Jesus was not understood on the day after the Crucifixion. It took several decades to get it all sorted out and known throughout the Church (roughly 30-60 AD). The revelation to Paul, and his subsequent ministry, were necessary to make known the fullness of Jesus' message, which the disciples did not understand during Jesus' earthly ministry, and which some of them surely learned later from Paul. Paul was not merely "the thirteenth apostle." He was in many ways the first apostle.

Fourth, Matthew's *Sayings of Our Lord* did not present *who* Jesus Christ is. The Gospels of Luke and Matthew open with genealogy and nativity stories of Jesus that demonstrate His Davidic lineage, His miraculous birth, and the extraordinary signs and events that attended His birth. Epiphanius states that Matthew's Hebrew gospel lacked this material, and the fact that the Ebionites, who used *The Sayings* and the Old Testament as their Scriptures, denied Jesus' extraordinary birth, messiahship, and divinity, is further evidence that *The Sayings* didn't contain this material. *The Sayings* lacked this material because the Apostle Matthew was martyred before Paul's ministry and had an inadequate understanding of who Jesus Christ is. *The Sayings'* wholly inadequate presentation of who Jesus Christ is, is further proof that it is not inspired Scripture.

Fifth, it is often said that when the Church finalized the canon in the fourth century, apostolic authorship was one of the standards used in determining whether a writing was to be considered Scripture. *The Sayings of Our Lord* shows that a writing, even a gospel, may indeed have been written by an apostle, yet not be Scripture. The Apostle Matthew was present during most of Jesus' ministry, but did not have a full understanding of Jesus' message. Knowledge of "the facts" is not enough -- and the Apostle Matthew didn't even have all the facts. (And note the likely presence of a certain amount of troublesome or questionable material in *The Sayings*.) In order for a writing to be Scripture, its human author had to have been inspired by the Holy Spirit.

4. The verdict

Because *The Sayings* lacked the power of Scripture (which comes from the Holy Spirit), it wasn't used by the Church after about 70 AD and didn't become one of the Church's accepted writings. The fourth-century Church councils that finalized the canon didn't even consider *The Sayings*. The methodology of those Church councils may have been flawed in some ways, but their decisions were correct because God was in control.

The verdict is very clear: *The Sayings of Our Lord* is not the inspired Word of God.

5. A final thought

Finally, there is the argument that those parts of *The Sayings* that were used in tact in the canonical gospels (that is, where the canonical gospels used the exact wording given in *The Sayings*) were themselves inspired, so that the text of *The Sayings* contains both inspired verses and uninspired verses. Augustine, in answering whether the *Book of Enoch* is inspired scripture because its first sentence is quoted in Jude 14-16, opined that parts of *Enoch* are inspired -- the parts quoted in the New Testament. I disagree. The *Book of Enoch* is not inspired scripture. And its first sentence is not inspired when it is in the *Book of Enoch*, but becomes inspired when it is used in the New Testament because the Holy Spirit is using it to convey divine meaning. Likewise for material from the *Book of Jasher, Annals of King David*, etc. used in the Old Testament historical books, and for quotations from classical Greek literature used by Paul in his epistles. Thus material from *The Sayings* used with exact wording in the canonical gospels becomes inspired scripture in those gospels because the Holy Spirit is using it to convey God's message.

CHAPTER 20

The Sayings and the Synoptic Gospels

Let us now review the relationship between *The Sayings* and the synoptic gospels.

1. *The Sayings of Our Lord*

Matthew, who was probably the only one of the Apostles who could read and write, must have begun writing down Jesus' sayings (*logia*) early on. After a while he began adding parables, dialogues, and short incidents. Later it appears he placed the *logia* after the chronological narrative. He wrote in Aramaic and eventually his writing (or at least the first half of it) came to resemble a stripped-down version of the Gospel of Matthew, generally but not exactly in the same order, and lacking the genealogy/ nativity. His sources were his own memory and probably the memories of other Apostles and followers -- but he wasn't guided by the Holy Spirit.

Twelve years after the Crucifixion (about 40 AD), as he was leaving Jerusalem to do missionary work abroad, Matthew gave the Jerusalem Church a presentation copy of his writing, which he called *The Sayings of Our Lord*. This was the first Christian writing and it was commonly called "the Gospel" or "the Gospel of our Lord." In the following years there were many amateur translations of *The Sayings* into Greek. The *Didache*, compiled about 60 AD, quotes *The Sayings* many times, and even opens with a passage from *The Sayings* ("love your enemies").

2. *The Gospel of Mark*

After Peter was martyred in Rome in 64 AD, his interpreter Mark wrote the Gospel of Mark. In his gospel, Mark combined what he remembered Peter saying about Jesus' ministry with material from *The Sayings*. *The Sayings* may have provided Mark with some of the framework for his gospel. Mark began his gospel with the same "John baptizing in the Jordan" segment that opened *The Sayings*.

It is likely that Mark used much material from *The Sayings*, possibly most of it, but modifying it based on Peter's account of events. For example, Mark used *The Sayings*' story of the Rich Young Man largely intact. One story-telling difference is that, while in *The Sayings* the rich young man simply approaches Jesus, Mark has the young man running up to Jesus and kneeling before Him, details that probably came from Peter. In some places Mark polishes *The Sayings*' sometimes-rough wording, as when he omits the part about the young man "scratching his head." Mark probably modified other material that he took from *The Sayings* in the same way.

More importantly, Mark's account of the Rich Young Man contained essential Christian teachings that were absent from *The Sayings*. First, Mark's account explains that if the rich young man gives his possessions to the poor he will have treasure in heaven, which *The Sayings* did not do. And second, Mark's account adds that the rich young man must also "take up the cross" (undergo deprivation and persecution) in order to follow Jesus.

The changes that Mark makes present Jesus' teachings more fully than *The Sayings* does. *The Sayings* records Jesus' advice to the rich young man to give his wealth to the poor without explaining its significance and spiritual reward, and lacks Jesus' statement that personal sacrifice is required in order to be one of His followers. *The Sayings* account is spiritually thin, while Mark's version is eye-to-eye with Jesus. It is likely that throughout *The Sayings* events were recounted with little or no explanation of their real significance. Mark, on the other hand, wrote with the guidance of the Holy Spirit.

3. The Gospel of Luke

The Gospel of Luke appeared next, about 70 AD. Luke was an associate of Paul who accompanied him on some of his travels. Luke, who said there were several accounts before his, based his gospel on the Gospel of Mark, *The Sayings*, and information from other members of the Church. He begins his gospel with a genealogy (Luke 1) and nativity (Luke 2), then recounts the "John baptizing in the Jordan" segment that had opened *The Sayings* and the Gospel of Mark (Luke 3). Luke chapters two and three are significant expansions of *The Sayings*' brief opening segment.

Luke's nativity included both Jesus and John the Baptist, and spoke of John's parents Zachariah and Elisabeth, who also appeared in *The Sayings*' opening segment. Although Luke's tale of Zachariah and Elisabeth was likely suggested by *The Sayings'* reference to them, *The Sayings* itself appears to have only mentioned their names, without telling their important story or relating its significance. Luke's narrative, on the other hand, is dynamic and projects the auspiciousness of John's coming ministry, declaring it the fulfillment of prophecy. Luke's account was inspired by the Holy Spirit.

Luke's gospel also contained *The Sayings'* "love your enemies" segment. Luke's passage is closely related to that in *The Sayings*, both in contents and order. In *The Sayings*, the order of verses is ABCDEF. Luke's order is ACDFE-GR-B. Luke's version of verse B changes *Gentiles* to *sinners* to avoid offending the Gentiles who were the majority of Paul's followers. He also condenses verse B2 ("love those that hate you, and you will have no enemy") into "love your enemies" and places it at the beginning of verse A -- which is appropriate because it is the theme of the passage. Luke's version of "love your enemies" is a better statement of that theme than *The Sayings'* version is.

Finally, Luke told the story of the Rich Young Ruler. In general his account is close to that of Mark, but he rejects Mark's expanded opening ("there came one running, and kneeled to Him, and asked...") and uses *The Sayings'* simple opening instead. The Gospel of Luke is thus dependent on both the Gospel of Mark, *The Sayings*, and the Holy Spirit.

4. *The Gospel of Matthew*

The Gospel of Matthew appeared next, perhaps about 75 AD. It was written not by the Apostle Matthew, but by an unknown person whom scholars call the Mattheist, who based his gospel on *The Sayings* and the Gospels of Mark and Luke, and possibly other sources. It is called the Gospel of Matthew because it probably incorporates almost all of Matthew's *Sayings* (re-written and re-arranged, of course).

The Gospel of Matthew includes "love your enemies" and the Rich Young Ruler, both of which are based on the two previous synoptic versions, *The Sayings* original, and the Holy Spirit. The Mattheist's use of *Sayings* material is similar to that of Mark and Luke, but there is one verse that stands out because it expresses Jesus' will for us so well (i.e., it exemplifies the guidance the Holy Spirit gave to the Mattheist in using *Sayings* material). Here it is:

Sayings verse 1:3b (using the *Didache's* verse number) says, *Bless those that curse you, and pray for your enemies, and fast for those that persecute you.*

This is re-written in Matt 5:44 as *Love your enemies, bless them that curse you, do good to them that hate you, and pray for them which despitefully use you, and persecute you.* In this the Mattheist adds the commandment to *do good to them that hate you. The Sayings'* instructions to *bless, pray for* and *fast for* are things that don't involve confronting or having direct contact with those who oppose you. It's the easy way of handling the situation. Matt 5:44 adds the commandment to *do good to them.* This is a difficult thing to do because it involves humbling yourself, and replacing love of self with love for others. It means doing something good to someone who *hates* you, and that's much more difficult. But it's what Jesus wants us to do. The Mattheist has voiced a higher level of obedience and service desired by the Lord: *to love your neighbor as yourself in spite of his bad treatment of you.* This verse was fashioned by the Holy Spirit.

5. *The targums*

Let us now turn to another matter. There is a strong possibility that when the Apostle Matthew quoted the Old Testament in *The Sayings*, he didn't use the Masoretic Text or the Septuagint. Instead, he used an Aramaic *targum.* There are many places where the *targums* contain readings identical with (or very close to) an Old Testament quotation in the New Testament, which is different from the reading found in the Masoretic Text or the Septuagint.

For example, in Mark 4:12 Jesus paraphrases Isaiah 6:9-10 as follows: "...that seeing they may see and not perceive, and hearing they may hear and not understand, lest at any time they should be converted and their sins should be forgiven them." Only the *Isaiah Targum* says *forgive*: the Masoretic Text and the Septuagint both say *heal.* Jesus' wording of Isaiah 6:10 comes from a *targum* version that would have been read in a first-century synagogue (and would therefore have been familiar to Matthew and the other Apostles).

However, this does not mean that the *targums* stand behind <u>only</u> those New Testament (or synoptic gospel) verses where the text is different from that of the Masoretic Text or the Septuagint. Most of the time the *targum* text is identical with that of the Masoretic Text or the Septuagint. This means that the *targums* may stand behind all the Old Testament quotations in the New Testament (or in the synoptic gospels). And since Jesus and the Apostles and Peter's interpreter Mark all spoke Aramaic, and Matthew wrote *The Sayings* in Aramaic, it is very likely that the *targums* stand behind

<u>all</u> the Old Testament quotations in *The Sayings* and in the New Testament (or in the synoptic gospels).

6. Summary

In summary, *The Sayings of Our Lord*, written by the Apostle Matthew twelve years after the Crucifixion, was first Christian writing and the primary literary source upon which the synoptic gospels were based. The first of these, the Gospel of Mark, written by Peter's interpreter John Mark, drew its basic structure and much of its material from *The Sayings*. The next gospel, that of Luke, did not merely repeat *Sayings* material from Mark, but took additional material from *The Sayings* that Mark hadn't used. The third synoptic gospel, called that of Matthew but actually written by a gospelist called the Mattheist, also drew material directly from *The Sayings*, in addition to using the two previous gospels. All three synoptic gospels were written with the guidance of the Holy Spirit, which *The Sayings* was not, and presented Jesus' teachings more fully than *The Sayings* had. Finally, it is likely that *The Sayings* used the Aramaic *targums* for quoting the Old Testament, and passed these *targum* quotations into the synoptic gospels.

CHAPTER 21

Adios to Q!

We must now address another theory relating to the origin of the gospels, a theory that conflicts with the premise of the present book. It goes like this: In the Middle Ages the Church taught the Augustinian explanation of the gospels' origin: that the four gospels were written in the order in which they appear in the New Testament (first Matthew, then Mark, then Luke, then John) and that each was based on the ones before it. But in early modern times Bible scholars became aware that three of the gospels (Matthew, Mark and Luke, called the synoptic gospels) told much the same story, a different story from that in the Gospel of John. These three gospels have much common text that overlaps in ways that is sometimes difficult to explain. By comparing the order of pericopes (short units of material) in each of the synoptics, Karl Lachmann proved in 1835 that Mark was the first to be written and served as the basis for the other two. This is called *Markan priority.*

1. Brief history of the Theory of Q

In 1838 C.H. Weiss proposed the existence of a *second source*, Q (from the German word *Quelle*, meaning *source*), to explain the large amount of material common to Matthew and Luke (about 235 verses). Q is defined as all that material which is common to the Gospels of Matthew and Luke, but not found in the Gospel of Mark (nor in the Gospel of John, since John isn't a synoptic gospel). According to the 2-Source Hypothesis, Mark and Q were the first two gospels and were written independently, while Luke and Matthew were written later and each used both Mark and Q.

Most of Q consists of sayings of Jesus. In the late 19th century German scholars attempted to determine what the Q document looked like, how it originated, and how it was used in Matthew and Luke. Luke's version of Q material is generally considered to be closer to Q's original form than that in Matthew. In the early 20th century the theory of Q came to England, where it was championed by the renowned scholar B.H. Streeter. (Streeter refined the theory by postulating two additional minor sources, L and M, resulting in what is called the 4-Source Hypothesis.) Q theory soon came to America, where in recent decades it has been transformed in disturbing ways, ways which are now widely taught in American seminaries and universities.[47]

2. Reconstructions of Q

There have been several scholarly reconstructions of Q, which differ in such matters as the order of material, whether the Lucan or Matthean form of a verse is preferred, etc. John Kloppenborg's 1988 reconstruction, given in *Q Parallels*, emerged in the early 1990s as the established text for Q in America. Kloppenborg's reconstruction postulates several versions or strata of Q (designated as Q^1, Q^2, and Q^3) corresponding to progressive stages of its development. The oldest layer, Q^1, consists of sapiential instruction. The second layer, Q^2, announces judgment. The last layer, Q^3, includes later additions such as the Temptation in the Wilderness and certain other material. These layers were supposedly created by a "Q community", an early Christian social group that cherished and collected Jesus' sayings and further developed them in response to changing conditions. (A similar project, the Jesus Seminar held in 1985, sought to identify which of Jesus' sayings were "authentic"!)

3. International Q Project

In 1989 the International Q Project was organized under the auspices of the Society of Biblical Literature, and directed from the Claremont Graduate School in Claremont, California, two of the nation's most prestigious religious institutions. The Project sought "to establish and maintain a critical text of the Sayings Gospel Q" through a series of work sessions involving New Testament scholars from around the world. After the Project's completion in 1996, its editorial board began preparations

---

47 According to an alternative explanation, the Griesbach Hypothesis, Matthew was written first, then Luke, and the last of the three, Mark, was a summary of the first two. In 1964 William Farmer expanded Griesbach's idea into the 2-Gospel Hypothesis. A big problem with the Griesbach/2-Gospel Hypothesis is that it doesn't address the strong evidence for Markan priority. (Although in actuality, Mark's order of pericopes/events was probably based on that in *The Sayings*.)

to publish a one-volume *Critical Edition of Q* and a 31-volume series, *Documenta Q*, to be issued over several years. The 31-volume series offers "reconstructions of Q through two centuries of gospel research, excerpted, sorted and evaluated." In the introduction to *The Critical Edition of Q* (published in 2000), project director James M. Robinson labored to discredit Papias's statement on *The Sayings* by setting forth a large number of statements by scholars against it.

4. Q is being used to attack traditional Christianity

Currently Q is one of the hottest areas of New Testament research. Unfortunately, this research has been used to undermine traditional Christianity. The major Q theorist, John Kloppenborg, claims that Q was created by "the people of Q" who based it on the "ancient wisdom collections" of the Babylonian, Egyptian, and Greek religions, and that Q is also related to certain Gnostic writings (see Kloppenborg, *The Formation of Q*, 2003). This means that a large part of the Gospels derive not from Jesus and the Apostles, but from pagan religions.

Another major Q theorist, Burton Mack, writes in his book *The Lost Gospel: The Book of Q and Christian Origins* (1993) that studying the Q document without reference to the gospels leads to the suspicion that "the people of Q were not Christians" and they "did not think of Jesus as a messiah" (both p. 48), that "Jesus was much more like a Cynic-teacher than either a Christ-savior or a messiah" (p. 245), and that Q "provide[s] evidence for a revised history of Christian beginnings that does not agree with the traditional Christian imagination based on the gospels" (p. 246). See also certain writings by James M. Robinson, co-chair of the International Q Project.

Other scholars have joined Q with the *Gospel of Thomas* as evidence that Christianity was the product of first-century religious trends (mystery, wisdom and savior cults) rather than the message of Jesus Christ. The implication is that Jesus was a Gnostic guru or wandering wisdom-teacher in the Cynic tradition -- not the Messiah and the Son of God!

5. Evidence that the Theory of Q is false

Evidence put forth in the present work demonstrates that the theory of Q is false, both in general and in its recent anti-Christian variations. Regarding the general form of Q Theory, Matthew's *Sayings* (the Hebrew gospel) cannot be Q, because Q *by definition* consists solely of material common to Matthew and Luke, while *Sayings* material such as the story of the Rich Young Ruler and the account of John the Baptist's ministry are found in all three synoptics. If one were to counter this by expanding the range of Q to include *Sayings* or Triple Tradition material, the expanded body of Q material would derail Kloppenborg's Q strata hypothesis (Q[1], Q[2], and Q[3]) and contradict Mack's "Jesus the Cynic-teacher" fantasy. (And the Q-*Thomas* hypothesis is dead because Gnostic *Thomas* isn't a first-century work.)

And there are others who disagree with Kloppenborg and Mack. In his book *Q and the History of Early Christianity* (1996), Oxford professor Christopher Tuckett expresses strong reservations about stratification theories, arguing that the Son of Man sayings "appear embedded in Q at all stages" and "present a remarkable homogeneity and consistency." Tuckett holds that Q isn't primarily a wisdom collection -- Adios, Q[1]! -- and that preaching about "this generation", which Kloppenborg calls a later addition, is actually one of Q's central aims. Such research is much needed.

6. The present writer hopes to destroy the Theory of Q

In summary, the theory set forth in the present book concerning Matthew's *Sayings of Our Lord* conflicts with the Theory of Q. The Theory of Q holds that the hypothetical document Q, not mentioned by any early Christian writer, was the source for much of the Gospels of Matthew and Luke. Q has been used to undermine the New Testament by claiming that much of the gospels are based on pagan writings rather than on the teachings of Jesus. The present theory, on the other hand, holds that Matthew's *Sayings of Our Lord*, whose existence is well attested by many early Christian writers, was the major document lying behind all three synoptic gospels -- and that Q doesn't exist. *The Sayings* was written by an eyewitness to Jesus' ministry and its use as a source for the synoptic gospels was guided by the Holy Spirit and is therefore true and correct. The present writer hopes that this book will contribute to the disappearance of the Theory of Q, and set the foundation for a new theory which is both historically and theologically correct.

CHAPTER 22

Impact on our Understanding of the New Testament

The present work's study of *The Sayings of Our Lord* and the Jewish Christians who used it has great impact on our understanding of the New Testament and the first-century Church. *The Sayings of Our Lord* radically re-writes the story of the New Testament Gospels.

1. Previous story of the synoptic gospels

Previously, the story of the synoptic Gospels went, briefly, something like this: The Gospel of Mark was written first and is primarily the memoirs of the Apostle Peter as set down by his interpreter, Mark. The Gospel of Luke was written next, by Paul's companion Luke, who took a large amount of material from Mark's Gospel, and used other sources. Finally, the Gospel of Matthew was written by the Apostle Matthew, who made use of both Mark's account and the Gospel of Luke, and other sources.

The Gospels of Mark, Luke and Matthew were also inspired by the Holy Spirit, which means that the human authors were assisted and guided by God in writing the Gospels. In addition, there is the considerable amount of material common to Matthew and Luke, that many say comes from the hypothetical document Q, the theory of which has been widely taught in recent decades.

2. New story of the synoptic gospels

The Sayings of Our Lord completely changes our understanding of how the synoptic gospels emerged. The new story goes like this: The first Gospel was *The Sayings of Our Lord*, written by the Apostle Matthew a dozen years after the Crucifixion, and consists of his own memories of the sayings and doings of Jesus. About 25 years later Mark wrote his Gospel, which combines Peter's oral account with material from *The Sayings*. Next appeared the Gospel of Luke, which used material from both *The Sayings* and the Gospel of Mark, and from other sources. Last appeared the Gospel of Matthew, which took material from *The Sayings* and the Gospels of Mark and Luke, and from other sources. The last three Gospels (but not *The Sayings*) were inspired by the Holy Spirit. Among other things, this means that the Holy Spirit guided the human authors of the synoptic Gospels in how to use material taken from *The Sayings*. Finally, there was no "Q".

This is a radical revision of the history of Scripture that brings the Gospel accounts closer to Jesus' ministry. The facts about *The Sayings* shows that the synoptic Gospels were based on an eyewitness account of Jesus' life and ministry (there is no evidence that Mark, Luke or the Mattheist knew Jesus) and thus supports the truth of the Gospel accounts of Jesus' life. *The Sayings* also gives the Gospels a basis involving good historical grounding and normal literary processes. This makes the Gospels more credible.

3. Other impacts on our understanding of the NT

And there are many other ways in which knowledge of *The Sayings* impacts our understanding of the New Testament and the early Church. Major facts, concepts, and explanations brought out by this work include the following:

1. There was another gospel before "Matthew, Mark, Luke, and John." A "lost gospel" that's been forgotten. A gospel that was written by one of the Apostles, the real Matthew.

2. *The Sayings* was the basis for Matthew, Mark, and Luke (the synoptic gospels), and provided their common material (called the *triple tradition*). The synoptic gospels are very similar not because Matthew and Luke are based on Mark, but because all three are based on *The Sayings*. The literary relationships between the synoptic gospels will need to be re-studied and revised.

3. It shows that the Gospels were based on an eyewitness account of Jesus' life and ministry. This supports the truth of the Gospel accounts of Jesus' life. (Dating the Gospels at 60 to 90 AD puts a big gap in the historical record. *The Sayings* was written 12 years after the Crucifixion.)

4. It gives the Gospels a basis involving good historical grounding and normal literary processes (for the benefit of rationalists and skeptics, and those Christians who believe that God usually works through natural mechanisms). This makes the Gospels more credible -- not works of fiction.

5. It gives us a better understanding of the literary processes by which the Gospels were produced.

6. It explains why some Scripture quotations in the Gospels come from the Aramaic *targums* (a fact known only to specialists) rather than from the Masoretic Text or the Septuagint.

7. It gives us a better understanding of the nature of divine inspiration, and its role in creating the New Testament.

8. It supports the importance of the *Didache* for understanding first-century Christianity.

9. It shows the falsehood of theories that the Gospels were based on ancient wisdom collections and/or material from other ancient religions, such as Orphism or Zoroastrianism.

10. In particular, it shows the falsehood of the Theory of Q.

4. Better understanding of history and literary processes

Again, the major impact of the ideas put forth in this book is that they give us a better understanding of the <u>historical events</u> and the <u>literary processes</u> involved in the creation of much of the New Testament. The story of *The Sayings of Our Lord* and Jewish Christianity will allow us to construct a much fuller account of how Christianity began and how it developed in the first century. The creation and reliability of the Gospels are crucial in this.

There has long been skepticism about how the Gospels were created: *How could illiterate fishermen have written the Gospels? How could they have been written so many years after the Crucifixion? If Jesus and the disciples spoke Aramaic, and the Gospels were written in Greek, who really wrote them? How do we know the Gospels are reliable? If Mark, Luke, and the Mattheist were not eyewitnesses to Jesus' ministry, how do we know that what they wrote is true?* This book seeks to provide logical answers to these and similar questions in order to help those who need a reason to believe, who have doubts, or whose faith is wavering. It is hoped that information in the present work will be of use in future books, articles, and dissertations that seek to defend and promote the Gospel.

Let God's truth be known to all!

APPENDIX A

The Aramaic Language

1. Semitic language family

Aramaic is a member of the Semitic language family. A language family is a group of languages that descend from a common mother-language and have related vocabulary and grammar. English, for example, is a member of the Indo-European language family, which includes most of the languages spoken in Europe, Iran and northern India. The English word *mother* is cognate to the German word *mutter*, the Latin *mater*, the Greek *meter*, the Russian *mat'*, etc., all of which mean *mother*.

THE WORLD'S MAJOR LANGUAGE FAMILIES

Indo-European (spoken in Europe, Iran, India, and parts of Central Asia), major languages include English, French, Spanish, German, Russian, Farsi, and Hindi. Since 1500 English, French and Spanish have spread to many places across the world.

Ural-Altaic (spoken in northern Russia, Central Asia, and Mongolia), major languages include Turkish, Mongolian, Finnish, and Hungarian.

Sino-Tibetan (spoken in China, Tibet, and southeast Asia), major languages include Mandarin Chinese, Wu (Cantonese), Tibetan, Thai, and Burmese.

Semitic (spoken in North Africa and the Near East), major languages include Arabic, Hebrew, and Amharic.

Niger-Congo (spoken in central Africa), major languages include the Bantu languages (including Swahili).

Malayo-Polynesian (spoken in insular Southeast Asia and the central and southern Pacific), includes Malay, Tagalog (the Philippines), Hawaiian, Samoan, Fijian, Maori (New Zealand), and Malagasy (Madagascar).

The world's major language-families are Indo-European, Semitic, Ural-Altaic, Sino-Tibetan, Niger-Congo, and Malayo-Polynesian. The modern Semitic languages include Modern Hebrew, Modern Arabic, South Arabic, Maltese, Amharic, Tigré, Tigrinya, and several others. Ancient Semitic languages include Babylonian, Assyrian, Phoenician, Ancient Hebrew, Aramaic, Classical Arabic (the language of the Koran), Ge'ez, and a few others.

SEMITIC LANGUAGES

Ancient Languages
  Northeastern Branch:
    Old Akkadian, Babylonian, Assyrian
  Northwestern Branch:
    Aramaic Group: Biblical Aramaic, Samaritan, Nabatean, Syriac, Mandaean
    Canaanite Group: Old Canaanite, Moabite, Old Hebrew, Ugaritic, Phoenician (including Punic and Carthaginian)
  Southern Branch:
    South Arabic (Mineo-Sabean), Ge'ez (in Ethiopia), Classical Arabic (the language of the Koran)

Modern Languages
    Modern Standard Arabic (the Cairo dialect, used in the media in all Arab countries), Modern Arabic dialects, Modern Hebrew, Amharic (in Ethiopia), Maltese

---

2. Origin of Aramaic

Aramaic was the language of the Arameans, who settled in Syria (called *Aram*, meaning *highlands*) about 2000 BC or earlier. About 800 BC they began to play a prominent role in the revived Assyrian Empire, and continued that role in the succeeding Neo-Babylonian (Chaldean) Empire. Their language was used as the official language -- called Imperial Aramaic -- of the Neo-Assyrian and Chaldean Empires, and the western half of the Achaemenian (Persian) Empire. Aramaic was widely spoken in the Near East for over 2000 years and was the region's *lingua franca* for much of that time.

3. Early Jewish use of Aramaic

The Northern Kingdom (Israel) was captured by the Assyrians in 721 BC, and its people were deported to Babylonia (central Mesopotamia). In 586 BC the Southern Kingdom (Judea) was captured by the Chaldeans (who had replaced the Assyrians) and its people were also deported to Babylonia. In 538 BC the Jews were returned to Palestine by the Persians (who had replaced the Chaldeans), except that ten tribes didn't return, the Ten Lost Tribes. During the Babylonian Captivity, the Jews began using Babylonian Aramaic as their daily language and restricted the use of Hebrew to religious services and other formal activities.

About 99% of the Old Testament is written in Hebrew, but there are two moderately long passages written in Aramaic, Daniel chapters 2 through 7 and most of Ezra 4 through 7. The Aramaic chapters of Daniel were written about 600 BC in Imperial Aramaic. The Hebrew chapters of Daniel were written about 165 BC, based on internal evidence. Ezra, written about 450 BC, is also in Imperial Aramaic. The Aramaic of Daniel and Ezra is also called Biblical Aramaic.

4. Middle and Late Aramaic

The language from 300 BC to 200 AD is called Middle Aramaic. The Torah (Genesis through Deuteronomy) was translated into Middle Aramaic about 200 BC. Later most of the rest of the Old Testament was translated into Middle Aramaic, but in sections rather than as one whole book. These Middle Aramaic translations of sections of the Old Testament are called *targums*. They were often read in synagogue after the Hebrew readings, which most people didn't understand.

Late Aramaic. the language from 200 AD to 900 AD, is divided into East Aramaic (in Mesopotamia, including the Aramaic of the Babylonian Talmud, called Jewish Aramaic) and West Aramaic (in Syria and Palestine). West Aramaic is divided into several dialects, including Galilean Aramaic, Samaritan Aramaic, and Christian Palestinian Aramaic.[48]

---

48 West Aramaic differs from East Aramaic in three main ways: 1) West Aramaic distinguishes definite nouns from indefinite nouns, while East Aramaic does not; 2) the plural of masculine nouns ends in -ayya in West Aramaic, while East Aramaic uses -ē; and 3) in imperfect tense verbs, the prefix for the third-person masc. is *yod* in West Aramaic (as in Hebrew), while East Aramaic uses either *nun* or *lamed*. There are also many minor differences. It is usually quite easy to tell whether a passage is written in East Aramaic or West Aramaic.

5. Aramaic grammar and vocabulary

Like European languages, Aramaic has nouns and verbs, singular and plural, present, past, and future tenses, etc. Verbs also have infinitive, imperative, and passive participle forms. But nouns, and second- and third-person verbs, also have gender (masculine and feminine). And when the object of a verb is a pronoun, it is usually expressed as a suffix to the verb (as in Spanish). Most possessive pronouns are also expressed by a suffix.

MAJOR LANGUAGES
SPOKEN BY THE JEWISH PEOPLE

Old Hebrew. The original language of the Jewish people; a Semitic language related to Phoenician and Aramaic. The Old Testament is written in Old Hebrew. There is a Jewish legend that Adam and Eve spoke Hebrew.

Aramaic. During the Babylonian Exile (721-540 BC) the Jews began to speak Aramaic instead of Hebrew. By 500 BC most Jews spoke Aramaic. Jesus and the Apostles spoke Aramaic. The large Jewish population of medieval Mesopotamia spoke Aramaic, and the Talmud, written 200-500 AD, is mostly in Aramaic. By about 1200 AD most Middle Eastern Jews spoke Arabic or Farsi.

Ladino. Jews in medieval Spain spoke Ladino, a form of Spanish with many Hebrew loan-words. After the Jews were expelled from Spain by the Inquisition in the 1490s, many Spanish Jews fled to north Italy and coastal Yugoslavia. Today Ladino is spoken only by a few Jews in Yugoslavia.

Yiddish. In the Middle Ages, Jews in Germany spoke Old Yiddish, a form of Old German with many Hebrew loan-words. About 1350 AD Jews in the Rhineland were invited to settle in Poland. They spread into Lithuania, western Russia, the Ukraine, and Hungary. East European Yiddish has many loan-words from East European languages. Most Yiddish-speakers died in the Holocaust.

Modern Hebrew. From the Middle Ages on Hebrew was a dead language and very few Jews lived in Palestine. In the 1870s European Jews began to settle in Palestine to create a Jewish homeland. They wanted to start speaking Hebrew also, but since the Old Testament and the Talmud didn't have many words for modern ideas and life (vaccine, telescope, Thailand), they created new words.

Most verbs have a tri-consonantal root (as in all Semitic languages). For example, the root form of the word *write* in Syriac is *k-t-b*. The verb is conjugated by changing the vowels in the word: *ketbet* means *I wrote* (common gender); *ktabn* or *ktabnan, we wrote* (common gender); *ktabt, you wrote* (common gender, sing.); *ktabtēn , you wrote* (fem. pl.); *ktabton, you wrote* (masc. pl.), etc. The normal word-order in a sentence is verb-subject-object (VSO), while in English it is subject-verb-object (SVO). Finally, while most of the grammar is very similar to Hebrew, the vocabulary of Aramaic is often very different from that of Hebrew, especially for commonly used words, such as *come, speak, see, go up, go down*, etc.

6. Aramaic alphabets

Originally the Arameans used the Phoenician alphabet, which has the same 22 letters as Hebrew. But about 750 BC they began developing their own variation of it, and by about 600 BC this had become the script in which Imperial Aramaic was written. About 200 AD, the dialect of East Aramaic spoken in Edessa (now Urfa, Turkey) had become the most widely-used language of Mesopotamian Christians. Known as Syriac, this language played a major role in the history of Near Eastern Christianity.

By about 400 AD the Aramaic alphabet had developed into the Estrangelo script (meaning "Gospel letters" because early on the *Diatessaron* was written in it), an exotic form of cursive writing still used for East Syriac today. From Estrangelo the Serto script was developed for the Western Syriac used by the Syrian Orthodox Church (Jacobites) in Syria, and the Chaldean script was developed for the Eastern Syriac used by the Nestorians in Mesopotamia, Persia, and south India.

At this same time (the Late Antiquity-Early Medieval era), the Jews in Babylonia, who were then creating the Babylonian Talmud, were using a script called Square Aramaic. This has been the standard Hebrew alphabet ever since and is the script in which Hebrew Bibles are printed today. About 100 BC, the Nabateans (the Arab inhabitants of Petra in southwest Jordan) began using a modified form of the Aramaic alphabet, in which many letters were rounded and letters were often joined together. By about 300 AD this had become the early Arabic alphabet.

7. Palestinian Aramaic written in the Old Hebrew alphabet

None of this was used to write Palestinian Aramaic in the first century AD. About 25% of the Dead Sea Scrolls -- written between 200 BC and 70 AD -- are in Aramaic. (The reason that 75% of the Dead Sea Scrolls are in Hebrew at a time when most Jews spoke Aramaic, is that most of the Dead Sea Scrolls are either copies of Old Testament books or other religious writings that were required to be in Hebrew.) The Aramaic Dead Sea Scrolls are written in the form of the Old Hebrew alphabet that was in use at that time. This is the script in which Palestinian Aramaic was written in the first century.

Like Hebrew, Aramaic is written from right to left (the opposite direction from how we write). What we think of as the last page of a book is actually the first page, and vice versa. As in ancient Hebrew, there was no punctuation and only slight spaces between words. Aramaic was also written without the diacritical marks (points written above and below the letters to indicate vowels, etc.) that are often used in medieval and modern Hebrew. One of the later Dead Sea Scrolls written in Aramaic would provide a good idea of what something written in Palestinian Aramaic in the first century AD looked like.

8. Jesus and the Apostles spoke Palestinian Aramaic

In the first century all Jews in Palestine spoke Aramaic (actually Palestinian Middle Aramaic) -- and most spoke nothing else. It was the language of the country. Merchants and those who dealt with the Romans spoke Aramaic and some Greek or Latin. Everybody else spoke Aramaic. Jesus and His disciples spoke Aramaic. (As the Eternal Word through Whom the world was created, Christ has all knowledge and knows all languages. But on the human side of the Incarnation,[49] Mary's son Jesus was fully human, had to learn to speak as a small child, and spoke only Aramaic.)

The Gospel of Mark gives Jesus' words in the original Aramaic in several places: *Boanerges* ("the sons of thunder") in Mk 3:17, *Talitha kumi* ("Maiden, arise!") in Mk 5:41, *Corban* ("gift [to God]") in Mk 7:11, *Ephphatha* ("Be opened!") in Mk 7:34, *Bartimeus* ("the son of Timeus") in Mk 10:46, *Abba* ("Father") in Mk 14:36, *Golgotha* ("the place of a skull)

---

49 God the Son is the second member of the Trinity, along with God the Father and the Holy Spirit. In his role as Savior, He took on human flesh, the Incarnation. The Gospel of John says, "And the Word was made flesh, and dwelt among us" (1:14). In the words of a Catholic catechism, "Jesus Christ is inseparably true God and true man."

in Mk 15:22, and *Eloi, Eloi, lama sabachthani?* ("My God, My God, why hast Thou forsaken Me?") in Mk 15:34.[50] All are in Aramaic.[51] The gospel was given to mankind in Aramaic.

9. The story of the Aramaic language since 100 AD

Let us say a few more things that are important to know about Aramaic and to explain the language gap between the first century and today. Early Christians in Syria and northern Mesopotamia used the Old Syriac versions of the New Testament and probably targums of the Septuagint Old Testament. About 160 AD Tatian created the *Diatessaron*, a harmony of the Gospels in Aramaic. About 400 AD Bishop Rabbula of Edessa created the *Peshitta*, the entire Bible in Syriac. The Nestorians carried the *Peshitta* (and Syriac) across Central Asia into China and Mongolia, where the Aramaic alphabet became the basis for the Uighur script in 800 AD and the Mongol script in 1200 AD. The major figures in Syriac religious literature include Ephraem Syrus (who flourished c. 350 AD), Aphraates (c. 325 AD), Jacob of Sarug (c. 500 AD), Barhebraeus (c. 1250 AD), and several others.

After the Muslim conquest of the Near East about 650 AD, Arabic slowly began to replace Aramaic as the daily language of the people. About 850 AD Aramaic scholars in Baghdad translated many ancient Greek philosophical and scientific writings into Arabic. Later in the Middle Ages these passed through Muslim Spain to France and Italy. The half-way point in the process of Arabic replacing Aramaic in the Near East occurred about 1400, when Tamerlane killed much of the population of Mesopotamia. (In Egypt, the half-way point for Arabic replacing Coptic was about 1300.)

Finally, Syriac is still the liturgical language of the Syrian Orthodox Church in Syria (very few of whose several million members understand because they all speak Arabic) and the liturgical language of most of the Christians in south India, whose church has been fragmented by Portuguese and British colonialism. Syriac is still spoken in several villages in southeastern Turkey (in Turkish Kurdistan and around Lake Urmia). And a dialect of West Aramaic very similar to Palestinian Aramaic is still spoken in a few villages near Damascus.

---

50 In addition, *Māranā tâ* ("Come, O Lord!" 1 Cor 16:22) is an Aramaic phrase used by early Christians, and *Abbâ* ("Father") also occurs in Rom 8:15 and Gal 4:6.

51 Matt 27:46 gives Jesus' final words on the Cross in Hebrew not because He spoke them in Hebrew (His actual words in Aramaic are given in Mk 15:34), but because He was quoting Psalm 22:1 (probably from an Aramaic targum) and the author of the Gospel of Matthew wished to give the quotation in the original Hebrew.

APPENDIX B

Melê De-Māran

The title of *The Sayings of Our Lord* in Greek may have been τὰ Λόγια τοῦ ἡμῶν Κυρίου (which transliterates as *tá Lógia toû hēmōn Kūriou*), but was more likely simply Λόγια τοῦ ἡμῶν Κυρίου, since the word *the* was usually omitted at the beginning of Greek titles. *Logia* is the plural of *logion*, which means a *saying*. *Logion* comes from the Greek word *logos*, whose basic meaning is *word*, and by extension *thought* or *idea*, and also means the *Word* of God (both the eternal Truth and the Word made flesh). *Hēmōn* means *our*. *Ta* and *tou* are forms of the word *the*, but the Greek rules for using the article are different than those of English. The word *kyrios* means *lord* and is the normal word for *Lord* (meaning Jesus Christ) in the Greek New Testament.

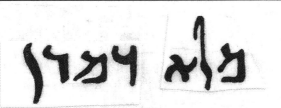

Melê de-Māran written in Old Hebrew letters of the first century, which the Apostle Matthew would have used.

The work's original Aramaic title was probably מלא דמרן, which transliterates as *Melê de-Māran*. The Aramaic word *melthā*, basically meaning *word*, is an irregular noun, being feminine in the singular (the Aramaic feminine ending *-thā* is cognate with the Hebrew feminine ending *-āt*) and masculine in the plural (the plural is *melê*). It has several meanings: 1) *word, saying, phrase, sentence, precept*, or *command*; 2) the *Logos* (the

Word of God); 3) *reason, the faculty of speech* or *thought*; 4) *proverb*. This range of meaning corresponds well with that of the Greek word *logos*.

Aramaic doesn't have a definite article and expresses the idea *the* differently than English does. The ending *ā* in the singular indicates that it is in the emphatic state (something like the nominative case in Indo-European languages, but only very roughly). The emphatic ending *ā* has a demonstrative force usually equivalent to the definite article *the*. Hence, *melthā* actually means *the word*. This also applies to the plural, so that *melê* means *the words*, or *the sayings*, or *the proverbs*, etc.

The word *d* (pronounced with a brief vowel sound, which varies according to the following letter) is a relative pronoun meaning *who, which*, or *that*. It is an inseparable particle prefixed to the noun which it modifies. In Aramaic there are three ways to indicate noun-to-noun possession (for example, *the man's horse* or *the Psalms of David*). In the method used here, the first noun (the thing possessed) is in the emphatic state. The second noun (the possessor) has the inseparable particle *d* prefixed to it. This is usually transliterated as *de-*.

The word *mār* has several meanings: 1) *master, ruler, prince*; 2) *sir* (in addressing a superior); 3) used as a title for saints and church dignitaries (as in the name of the famous monastery near Jerusalem, Mar Saba); 4) the *Lord* (God or Jesus). In the emphatic state it is only used for the Lord God, and represents the Tetragrammaton in the Aramaic Old Testament (the Peshitta, which also includes the New Testament). The suffix *-an* means *our* and corresponds with the Hebrew suffix -anū (-inū, -enū, etc.), which also means *our*. The Aramaic phrase *Māran ātha* (*Come, our Lord!*) occurs in 1 Cor 16 and Rev 22 and was a watchword of the first-century Church.

APPENDIX C

Scrolls and Codices

The most common writing material in the first century AD was the papyrus scroll. Papyrus is a large reed that grows in the swampy parts of the Nile delta. It grows six to twelve feet high out of the water, as thick as a man's arm, and the ancient Egyptians used it to make boats and other things. The Egyptians made papyrus sheets at least as early as 2400 BC.

To make a scroll, the pithy core is cut into thin strips about an inch wide and usually eight to twelve inches long (although dimensions varied). Eight or ten strips would be laid side by side into a square, and then eight or ten more were laid crosswise on top, and glued in place with paste or with the strips' own juices. The assembled sheet was then pounded and dried, and later smoothed with a flat stone or piece of ivory.

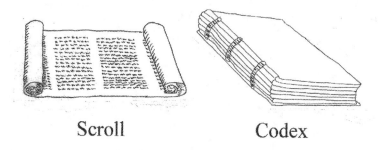

Scroll   Codex

About twenty finished sheets were overlapped slightly and glued together to form a long roll, usually about a foot wide and twenty feet long. Wooden handles were usually attached at each end. Alexandria, at the northwest corner of the Nile delta, was the center for producing papyrus scrolls and exporting them across the Mediterranean. This was the reason for the existence of the famous library at Alexandria.

Scrolls made out of leather were also used by the Greeks, Persians and

Hebrews early on. Although the Egyptians seldom used leather scrolls, the earliest surviving leather scroll is from Egypt, about 1500 BC. Sometime before 300 BC parchment appeared. Instead of tanning the animal-skin to produce leather, another process was used. The animal-skin was soaked in quicklime water, then scraped on both sides, dried, and rubbed with chalk or pumice-stone. This produced a smooth writing surface that was long-lasting. Parchment made from the skin of a calf or young goat is very fine and is called vellum. Sheets of parchment were sewn together to make parchment scrolls. The city of Pergamum (on the west coast of Turkey) was the center of parchment production from about 300 BC on.

Not long before the first century AD an early form of book appeared, the codex. The usual way to make a codex was to lay four sheets of papyrus (or parchment) on top of each other, then fold them in half and sew them together along the fold. This produced a quire with eight two-sided pages. A number of quires -- sometimes over a hundred -- were then stacked on top of each other in a binding cradle. Several holes were drilled through the stack about a half-inch from the sewn edge and a cord was threaded through it. A leather or wooden cover was then attached, completing the codex.

Although the codex probably appeared in the first century BC, it did not become widely used for some time. At first it was viewed as a type of notebook, and was used for business records, long letters, first drafts of various writings, and any kind of log into which periodic entries would be made. The scroll continued to be used for works of literature and formal records for several centuries.

Early on, however, Christians began to use the codex to record the Scriptures. One reason for this is that early Christians were constantly "searching the Scriptures" to find passages that related to their faith. Looking up widely-separated verses or passages in a scroll was a difficult and time-consuming process, especially since chapter and verse divisions were not introduced until the Middle Ages. The early Church is credited with popularizing the codex and eventually making it the standard format for literature.

APPENDIX D

Lamsa's Aramaic Bible

The reader is advised to beware of the Peshitta translation by George Lamsa entitled *The Holy Bible from Ancient Eastern Manuscripts* (originally published in 1957).[52] A little background: The Peshitta as created by Bishop Rabbula lacked five New Testament books that were disputed at that time: 2 Peter, 2 & 3 John, Jude and Revelation. (There was particular resistance to John's Revelation, which is said to have been unknown to the early Syrian Church. A number of independent translations of Revelation into Syriac appeared in the Middle Ages.) Although these five books were included in the Philoxenian revision of 508 AD and in the Harklean revision of 616 AD, they were not, and are not, part of the Peshitta and are not recognized by the Syrian Church. They are obscure scholarly texts which the average Syrian Christian has never seen.

Now, how this applies to the Lamsa translation: Lamsa claims that the New Testament was originally written in Aramaic (parts of it were) and that the Peshitta contains the original Aramaic New Testament. Not true! First, Jesus and His disciples spoke Palestinian Aramaic, a dialect of West Aramaic, while the Peshitta is written in Syriac, a dialect of East Aramaic. Second, scholars have proven (from grammatical constructions in the Peshitta) that the Peshitta's New Testament was translated from the Greek New Testament. Third, the Syrian Church has long held that the Peshitta was produced by Bishop Rabbula about 400 AD (probably in part by revising the Old Syriac versions).

---

52 George M. Lamsa was born in Kurdistan (probably in northern Iraq) in 1890. He came to America about 1920 and died in California in 1975. During his last decade he had an associate, Rocco A. Errico, who has continued his work at the Noohra Foundation in Smyrna, Georgia.

In addition, Paul Victor Wierwille, in whose Ohio home Lamsa completed his Peshitta translation, soon founded The Way International, a non-trinitarian Bible study organization which came to have hundreds of chapters nationwide. The organization uses Lamsa's Peshitta Bible and also publishes its own Peshitta and Syriac study materials.

In addition, the real Peshitta contains the Septuagint Old Testament (which means it contains the Apocrypha) and omits the five disputed New Testament books (2 Peter, 2 & 3 John, Jude, and Revelation). However, Lamsa brings his Peshitta translation into line with the Protestant canon by omitting the Septuagint's extra books and borrowing the missing New Testament books from a later Syriac translation. This appears to have been done so that readers wouldn't dismiss the Peshitta as an incorrect version of the Bible -- particularly the New Testament, which Lamsa is trying to convince his readers is the original New Testament.

Finally, his "translation" contains many startling readings (contradicting traditional theology at key points) that Aramaic scholars say are completely incorrect. If his readings were correct the teachings of the Syrian Church, which is a normal Christian church, would be very different!

As an example, let us examine Matt. 27:46, one of Jesus' last words on the Cross. The King James wording of this verse is "And about the ninth hour Jesus cried with a loud voice, saying, Eli, Eli, lama sabachthani? that is to say, My God, my God, why has thou forsaken me?" The traditional understanding of this relates to Psalm 22, whose first verse is "My God, my God, why hast thou forsaken me?"

Psalm 22 also contains many elements which predict the events of the Crucifixion: vv. 6-7 "I am... a reproach of men, and despised of the people. All they that see Me laugh Me to scorn: they shoot out the lip, they shake the head, saying, He trusted on the Lord that He would deliver Him: let Him deliver Him, seeing He delighted in Him"; vv. 14-16 "I am poured out like water, and all My bones are out of joint... My strength is dried up like a potsherd; and My tongue cleaveth to My jaws... the assembly of the wicked have inclosed Me: they pierced My hands and My feet"; and v. 18 "They part My garments among them, and cast lots upon My vesture."

The traditional understanding of Jesus' quotation of Psalm 22:1 is that the Father withdrew from Jesus for three days when He died and took on the sins of the world, because God the Father cannot be in the presence of sin. Matt 27:46 is a key verse for understanding the Atonement.

Lamsa, however, translates verse 46 like this, "And about the ninth hour, Jesus cried out with a loud voice and said, *Eli, Eli, lemana shabakthani!* My God, my God, for this I was spared (or This was my destiny)." Lamsa explains this in several ways. First, he denies that Jesus is quoting Psalm 22:1 (which Lamsa translates as "My God, my God, why hast thou let me to live?" in his rendition of the Psalms). He also ignores all the other material in Psalm 22 predicting the Crucifixion.

Second, Lamsa denies that God the Father would have departed from (forsaken) Jesus, arguing that God never abandons His followers, and that Jesus' words "Father, forgive them…" and "Father, into Thy hands I commend My spirit" (given in Luke 23) show that Jesus believed the Father was with Him. In this, Lamsa reveals his fundamental misunderstanding of Jesus Christ as God's *sole* instrument (which even excludes the Father and the Holy Spirit) for Atonement of sin.

Third, Lamsa claims that the correct Aramaic reading is "My God, my God, for this you have kept me" (or "spared me" or "reserved me"), coming from the root *shwaq* which means "to keep, reserve, leave, spare, forgive, allow, permit." He argues that Jesus had a deep awareness of the reason that He was being crucified, and that His cry was a shout of victory. He had fulfilled His destiny to die a martyr's death.[53]

In all this Lamsa reveals his ignorance of the meaning and purpose of the Crucifixion. While dying a martyr's death is not an insignificant thing, the purpose of Jesus' death was much greater: to take onto Himself and atone for the sins of the world. Jesus' act of witness was not His death, His whole life was His act of witness. His death was the next step: putting His highest teaching into action. Lamsa doesn't understand this.

There are a great, great many places in *The Holy Bible from Ancient Eastern Manuscripts* where there are similar mistranslations, often at places that shock or upset the reader with "new understandings" of the Biblical text. It appears to the present writer that the goal of Lamsa's mistranslations is to shock and upset people -- and to establish Lamsa as the great expositor who reveals the Bible's true meaning. (And, oh yeah, to make a lot of money in the process.)

---

53   See George Lamsa and Rocco Errico, *Aramaic Light on the Gospel of Matthew* (2000), pp. 346-52 regarding Matt 27:46.

APPENDIX E

Books Condemned by the Gelasian Decree

What books did the *Gelasian Decree* condemn? This information is not essential to the subject of the present writing, but since it is of interest to many readers and is very difficult to obtain -- the fullest work on the subject was published in German a hundred years ago, in 1912 -- the *Gelasian Decree*'s list of condemned works is given in English here. I have added the numbering, and other material put into the title (such as the original Latin wording) is given in brackets.

It should be stated that the *Decree* is not a complete list of rejected writings (which would include a great many more items). Rather, it is a selective list that combines the major rejected works with selected lesser rejected works which were damaging in particular ways. Focusing on the reasons why these lesser works were included in the *Decree* helps us better understand the issues facing the Roman Church of about 500 AD.

1) **The travelogue [*itinerarium*] under the name of the Apostle Peter, which is called the nine books of Saint Clement, apocryphal.** *The Travels of Peter.* Clement was the bishop of Rome about 100 AD. This work may have been written in the middle of the second century and was probably based on the now-lost *Preaching of Peter* (itself written about 100 AD). It was highly revered by the Ebionites and was the source for much material in the pseudo-Clementine literature.

2) **The acts under the name of the Apostle Andrew, apocryphal.** *The Acts of Andrew.* A lengthy epitome of this work by Gregory of Tours, c. 575 AD, has survived.

3) **The acts under the name of the Apostle Thomas, apocryphal.** *The Acts of Thomas* is the only one of the five primary romances (the acts of Peter, Paul, Andrew, Thomas, and John) that has survived in its entirety.

4) **The acts under the name of the Apostle Peter, apocryphal.** *The Acts of Peter.* Written before 200 AD, it was largely modelled after the *Acts of John*, but parts were based on earlier sources. Several portions have survived.

5) **The acts under the name of the Apostle Philip, apocryphal.** Two-thirds of the *Acts of Philip* survive. It has no unorthodox teachings, but relates some improbable events, including an account of slaying a dragon with a communion cup -- which is probably why it was condemned.

6) **The gospel under the name of Matthew, apocryphal.** This is a different writing than the canonical Gospel of Matthew. It is *The Sayings of Our Lord* written by the Apostle Matthew.

7) **The gospel under the name of Barnabas, apocryphal.** In addition to the Gnostic *Gospel of Barnabas* listed here in the Decree, another *Gospel of Barnabas* was written in the fourteenth century by an Italian convert to Islam.

8) **The gospel under the name of James the Less, apocryphal.** Possibly the *Book of James* (or *Protevangelium*), which is actually an infancy narrative.

9) **The gospel under the name of the Apostle Peter, apocryphal.** *The Gospel of Peter.* This book, which incorporated Greco-Roman mythology about the underworld/afterlife, was widely used in the early Church and shaped the common Christian vision of Hell for over fifteen hundred years -- a horrifying image that still frightens many people today.

10) **The gospel under the name of Thomas which the Manicheans use, apocryphal.** A copy of this work was found in Upper Egypt in 1945 and has been the subject of much investigation and many sensational claims. Foremost is the claim that the *Gospel of Thomas* is an record of Jesus' teachings dating from before the NT gospels. However, the fact that *Thomas* contains *logia* that twist some of Jesus' sayings in ways that support Gnosticism (such as *Logia* 22, 44, 62, 68, etc.) shows that it drew from the NT gospels and was written much later, since such borrowing assumes that Christianity was already widespread. And since *Thomas* was quoted by Hippolytus about 225 AD, but appears to have been unknown to Irenaeus (whose 5-volume work mainly concerned Gnosticism), about 180 AD, it was probably written about

200 AD -- far too late to be an original, independent, eyewitness account of Jesus' teachings. Although the *Gospel of Thomas* is a Gnostic work, Manicheanism incorporated Gnosticism into its syncretistic system and used many Gnostic writings.

11) **The gospels under the name of Bartholomew, apocryphal.** One of these may be the same as the *Questions of St. Bartholemew*, which has survived in several corrupt versions.

12) **The gospels under the name of Andrew, apocryphal.** Although many scholars say there is no evidence for the existence of a "Gospel of Andrew," I feel that the church officials who put together the *Gelasian Decree* had access to information not available today.

13) **The gospels which Lucianus forged, apocryphal.** The canonical gospels as altered by a certain Lucianus.

14) **The gospels which Hesychius forged, apocryphal.** The canonical gospels as altered by a certain Hesychius.

15) **The book concerning the Savior's infancy, apocryphal.** There were many writings on this subject in the early Church.

16) **The book concerning the Savior's birth and concerning Mary or the midwife, apocryphal.**

17) **The book which is called that of the shepherd, apocryphal.** *The Shepherd of Hermas.* This book, written 125-150 AD, was widely used by the early Church and today is classed with the Apostolic Fathers. The complete text survives and has been much studied.

18) **All the books which the Devil's disciple Leucius made, apocryphal.** The real (or fictitious) companion of the Apostle John, to whom is attributed the *Acts of John* and several other works.

19) **The book which is called the foundation [*Fundamentum*], apocryphal.** *The Foundation* is attributed to Manes, the founder of Manicheanism.

20) **The book which is called the treasury [*Thesaurus*], apocryphal.** *The Treasury* is attributed to Manes, the founder of Manicheanism.

21) **The book concerning *the story of* the daughters of Adam, from the Book of Jubilees [*leptogeneseos*], apocryphal.** The *Book of Jubilees* was also called "the Little Genesis" (*Lepte Genesis*). Adam's two daughters are mentioned in chapter four. The *Book of Jubilees*, written about 125

BC, was part of the body of literature called by scholars "the re-written Torah." These writings revised the stories of Genesis and the Israelites' settlement of Palestine in ways that suited the social, economic, and political needs of late Second Temple Judaism.

22) **The pastiche** [*cento*] **concerning Christ stitched together** [*conpaginatum*] **out of verses from Vergil, apocryphal.** Duplicated in item 56. Vergil's *Aeneid* was Rome's national epic and this pastiche was obviously created to claim that Rome's national epic contained prophecies of Christ.

23) **The book which is called the deeds of Thecla and Paul, apocryphal.** *The Acts of Thecla and Paul* is an episode from *The Acts of Paul*. It tells one of the most famous legends of the early Church, how Thecla was saved by a lioness from the other beasts in the arena.

24) **The book which is called that of Nepos, apocryphal.** Nepos was an Egyptian bishop about 250 AD. His book espoused Chiliasm.

25) **The book of proverbs written by heretics and fore-sealed** [*presignatus*] **under the name of Saint Sixtus, apocryphal.** (1) It is uncertain what *presignatus* meant; perhaps it was something like *verified* or *notarized*. The Romans had a public official called a *praesignator*, but we don't know what his duties were. (2) The *book of proverbs... under the name of Saint Sixtus* was probably the *Sentences of Sextus*, a collection of 104 Pythagorean-style aphorisms that was popular among Christians and pagans alike in the second and third centuries. Later Christians attributed it to the beloved Pope Sixtus II (about 260 AD), but it was written much earlier, since Origen quotes it. A copy of the *Sentences* was found with the Gnostic writings at Nag Hammadi.

26) **The revelation which is called that of Paul, apocryphal.** *Paul's Revelation*. Written about 375 AD, this work pretends to contain the unutterable things which the Apostle Paul heard. Most of the text survives.

27) **The revelation which is called that of Thomas, apocryphal.** *The Apocalypse of Thomas*. The few pages of this work which survive concern the end of the world.

28) **The revelation which is called that of Stephen, apocryphal.** *The Revelation of Stephen*. The title implies a vision seen by the first Christian martyr, Stephen, but the few surviving pages only relate a fanciful account of his martyrdom.

29) **The book which is called the passing [*transitus*] of Saint Mary, apocryphal.** The *Assumption of the Virgin* has survived in Greek, Latin, Syriac, Coptic, Arabic and Ethiopic versions.

30) **The book which is called the penitence of Adam, apocryphal.** The ancient book called *The Penitence of Adam* has not survived. There is a medieval manuscript at the Library of the Arsenal in Paris called the *Book of the Penitence of Adam*. But this manuscript contains many kabbalistic ideas and cannot be the work listed in the *Gelasian Decree*, unless it has been greatly altered.

31) **The book concerning a giant by the name of Ogias who is held by the heretics to have fought with a dragon after the Flood, apocryphal.** This is the *Book of the Giants*, part of the body of Enochic literature. A badly preserved copy of it has been found among the Dead Sea Scrolls. The book was later adopted by the Manicheans as part of their literature, and Manichean versions of it have been found as far away as central Asia.

32) **The book which is called the testament of Job, apocryphal.** The *Testament of Job* is a piece of intertestamental literature, written between 100 BC and 100 AD. It retells the story of Job, but adds and deletes much material from the account given in the Old Testament Book of Job, and adds new themes to the story.

33) **The book which is called the penitence of Origen, apocryphal.** This may be the writing known as the *Lamentum Origenis* or *Planctus Origenis*, which purports to be the lament or wailing written by Origen. The *Lamentum Origenis* is actually a work of fiction written by an unknown person attempting to belittle Origen.

34) **The book which is called the penitence of Saint Cyprian, apocryphal.** The *Penitence of St. Cyprian* has nothing to do with the famous St. Cyprian who was the bishop of Carthage about 250 AD. It is the autobiographical account of a former magician, Cyprian of Antioch, about his conversion to Christianity after his magical arts failed to have any impact on the faith of a young Christian woman whom he had been hired to put a spell on to make her love a certain pagan man.

35) **The book which is called the penitence of Jamnes [sic] and Mambres, apocryphal.** Pharaoh's magicians (Ex. 7:11) are named in 2 Tim. 3:8 as Jannes and Mambres. The Aramaic targum on Exodus says that as Moses and the Israelites were leaving Egypt, Pharaoh's

magicians converted to Judaism and accompanied them in the exodus (this might have been their penitence), but perished on the journey to the Promised Land. Origen says that there was a book called *The Book of Jannes and Mambres* which told of their deeds and that the statement in Paul's epistle was based on it. Chester Beatty Papyrus No. XVI contains a writing entitled *The Apocryphon of Jannes and Mambres the Magicians*, but it is not certain whether this is the same as the book listed in the *Gelasian Decree* or the work mentioned by Origen.

36) **The book which is called the fates of the Apostles, apocryphal.** No Greek or Latin text of this book has survived. However, about 900 AD the Anglo-Saxon poet Cynewulf wrote a 122-verse poem on this subject with the title *The Fates of the Apostles*. It is not known whether Cynewulf's poem is related to the ancient book.

37) **The book which is called the games [*lusa*] of the Apostles, apocryphal.** The meaning of *lusa* is uncertain; it may be a misspelling. *Muse* (musa), *praise* (laus), and *grave-plate* (from an Ibero-Celtic word) have also been suggested. Since other manuscripts give different readings, it seems that medieval scribes were also perplexed.

38) **The book which is called the canons of the Apostles, apocryphal.** The *Apostolic Canons* was an early Church document which claims it was created at an early Church council held at Antioch, no date given. (The original *Apostolic Canons* does not survive today. But a version of its text has been preserved in the *Apostolic Constitutions*, which was created about 375 AD. The *Apostolic Canons* must therefore have been created before 375 AD.) About 500 AD -- about the same time that the *Gelasian Decree* was written -- 50 of the *Apostolic Canons'* 85 canons were translated into Latin and incorporated into the body of Catholic church law. It is possible that the earlier *Apostolic Canons* was condemned in order to discredit the 35 canons which the Catholic Church rejected.

39) **The book of natural history [*liber physiologus*] written by heretics and fore-sealed [*presignatus*] under the name of Ambrosius the Blessed, apocryphal.** Probably St. Ambrose, Bishop of Milan from 374 to 397 AD. His book *Hexaemeron* ("The Six Days") gave an account of the six days of Creation that went into considerable detail regarding the creation of fish and animal life on days five and six, and served as the basis for later medieval bestiaries.

40) **Eusebius Pamphilus's history, apocryphal.** Abut 320 AD Emperor Constantine declared Christianity the official religion of the Roman Empire. He also created a new patriarchy at his capital Constantinople to be the head of the Christian Church (removing Rome from the top position it had enjoyed for the previous century or two) and treated the bishop of Rome as one of the lesser, subservient patriarchs in the new imperial Church system. Eusebius was a close ally of Constantine and Constantine's system was defended and celebrated in his *Church History*. (See the imperial letter to the "bishop of Rome" in Book 10, which treats the pope as a subordinate part of Constantine's church system.) But by 500 AD the Roman papacy, and Pope Gelasius in particular, was engaged in a power struggle with the patriarchy of Constantinople for supremacy, and viewed Eusebius as an enemy.

41) **The minor works [*opuscula*] of Tertullian, apocryphal.** Minor in the sense of *short*, not *of little importance*. Tertullian was an important church writer of about 200 AD from north Africa, one of the earliest Latin Fathers. He coined the word *trinity* (*trinitas* in Latin).

42) **The minor works [*opuscula*] of Lactantius or Firmianus, apocryphal.** Lucius Caelius Firmianus Lactantius, known as Lactantius, was an important church writer of about 300 AD. His major work was *The Divine Institutes*.

43) **The minor works [*opuscula*] of Africanus, apocryphal.** Sextus Julius Africanus, a native of Palestine, was a Christian historian of about 200 AD. He calculated that Jesus was born on March 21, 1 BC (according to our calendar). His now-lost historical writings, famous in antiquity, may have contained some material objectionable to the Church.

44) **The minor works [*opuscula*] of Postumianus and Gallus, apocryphal.** Sulpicius Severus, a Christian writer 400 AD, is best remembered for his life of St. Martin of Tours. Postumianus and Gallus were characters in one of his lesser writings, the *Dialogues*, which concerned the lives of monks in the Egyptian desert and broached the issue of homosexuality. Even in 500 AD the Church was concerned about its public image.

45) **The minor works [*opuscula*] of Montanus, Priscilla and Maximilla, apocryphal.** Montanus founded Montanism, an ascetic and apocalyptic movement, about 160 AD. Priscilla and Maximilla were his two female associates.

46) **The minor works [*opuscula*] of Faustus the Manichean, apocryphal.** About 290 AD Faustus of Milevis brought Manicheanism to the West and wrote a book that re-interpreted the New Testament to support Manicheanism. Augustine was one of his main followers at this time.

47) **The minor works [*opuscula*] of Commodianus, apocryphal.** A Christian Latin poet from north Africa who flourished about 250 AD. His works were condemned because his theology was Chiliast and Patripassianist.

48) **The minor works [*opuscula*] of the other Clement of Alexandria, apocryphal.** Not the famous Christian scholar who wrote *The Miscellanies*, etc.

49) **The minor works [*opuscula*] of Thascius the Cyprian, apocryphal.** The famous bishop of Carthage about 250 AD, known as Cyprian. Many of the writings attributed to him are of doubtful authenticity.

50) **The minor works [*opuscula*] of Arnobius, apocryphal.** Arnobius of Sicca, a Christian apologist from north Africa of about 300 AD, was the teacher of Lactantius. His major work, *Adversus Gentes* (or *Adversus Nationes*), was widely read because it defended Christians from the charge that their impiety (i.e., refusal to honor the Roman gods) was the cause of Rome's troubles. However, as a recent convert to Christianity who still had many pagan ideas, his work was filled with serious theological errors.

51) **The minor works [*opuscula*] of Tichonius, apocryphal.** Tichonius Afer was a north African Donatist of about 380 AD. His *Seven Rules of Interpretation* (for interpreting the Bible) was used by Augustine in *De doctrina christiana* and had great influence on Christian thinking for several centuries. Tichonius also wrote a commentary on Revelation using his rules, which interpreted Revelation spiritually rather than literally. This was probably the work listed in the *Decree*.

52) **The minor works [*opuscula*] of Cassianus, a priest of the Gauls [*presbyter Galliarum*], apocryphal.** *Galliarum* was often used with place-names in Provence, which was inhabited by Gauls but wasn't part of the Roman province Gallia. Possibly John Cassian, who founded two monasteries near Marseilles about 415 AD. His attack on Augustine's teaching on grace was later considered semi-Pelagian.

53) **The minor works** [*opuscula*] **of Victorinus Petabionensis, apocryphal.** The bishop of Pettau in Pannonia who was martyred under Diocletian in 304 AD. His works were condemned for Millenarianist tendencies.

54) **The minor works** [*opuscula*] **of Faustus of Riez in Gaul** [*Regiensis Galliarum*]**, apocryphal.** Faustus, who was bishop of Riez, a town east of Marseilles, about 480 AD, was a well-known defender of semi-Pelagianism.

55) **The minor works** [*opuscula*] **of Frumentius the Blind, apocryphal.** There are known to have been two bishops by this name -- one of Tubursico in Numidia, and the other of Telepte on Byzacena -- but little is known about either one of them.

56) **The pastiche** [*cento*] **concerning Christ stitched together** [*conpaginatum*] **out of verses from Vergil, apocryphal.** Duplicate of item 22.

57) **The letter of Jesus to Abgar, apocryphal.** *The Letter of Jesus to Abgar.* The alleged correspondence between Jesus and Abgar is part of the story of the mission of Thaddeus and the conversion of Edessa.

58) **The letter of Abgar to Jesus, apocryphal.** *The Letter of Abgar to Jesus.*

59) **The martyrdom** [*passio*] **of Cyricus and Julitta, apocryphal.** When used in connection with Christian martyrdom, *passio* means arrest, torture and execution. The story of the martyrdom of St. Julitta and her son St. Cyricus (remembered in the name of the town St.-Cyr, home of the French military academy) was considered fictitious even in antiquity.

60) **The martyrdom** [*passio*] **of Georgius, apocryphal.** The story of the martyrdom of St. George, the patron saint of England who was said to have slain a dragon, was considered fictitious even in antiquity.

61) **The writing** [*scriptura*] **which is called the exorcism** [*interdictio*] **of Solomon, apocryphal.** The title doesn't mean the story of an exorcism performed on Solomon, but rather a book about exorcism written by Solomon. The late Second Temple period legend that Solomon's great wisdom included knowledge of exorcism is expressed in detail in Josephus's *Antiquities* 8.5. The *Testament of Solomon* from about 200 AD, which claims to be written by Solomon and consists mostly of stories about the role of demons and magic in Solomon's life, and

which credits the major events in Solomon's life not to God but to the power of demons, is probably the book that the *Decree* condemns.

62) **All amulets [*phylacteria*] which have been inscribed not with the names of angels, as some people imagine, but with the names of sorcerer demons, apocryphal.** Praying to and venerating (worshiping?) angels was a major problem at this time, which led to the invention of hundreds of newly named angels. The Church responded by declaring that only the four angels named in the Catholic Bible could be invoked: Michael, Gabriel, Raphael and Uriel.

* * * * * * * * *

The *Decree* then gives the names, in roughly chronological order, of many individuals whose teachings and writings are condemned. Most of them were major heretics or schismatics in the early Church. I have added numbering to the list below, but have given no commentary.

1) Simon Magus; 2) Nicolaus; 3) Cerinthus; 4) Marcion; 5) Basilides; 6) Ebion; 7) Paul of Samosata; 8) Photinus and Bonosus who [both] erred in a similar way; 9) Montanus with his indecent followers; 10) Apollinaris; 11) Valentinus or Manicheus; 12) Faustus Africanus; 13) Sabellius; 14) Arrius; 15) Macedonius; 16) Eunomius; 17) Novatus; 18) Sabbatius; 19) Calistus; 20) Donatus; 21) Eustatius; 22) Jovinianus; 23) Pelagius; 24) Julianus Eclanensis; 25) Caelestius; 26) Maximianus; 27) Priscillianus from Spain; 28) Nestorius Constantinopolitanus; 29) Maximus the Cynic; 30) Lampetius; 31) Dioscorus; 32) Eutyches; 33) Peter and the other Peter, one of whom polluted Alexandria, and the other Antioch; 34) Acacius Constantinopolitanus.

APPENDIX F

The Titles of Certain Early Christian Writings

Clement of Alexandria. The Greek title of his major work is *Stromateis* (literally, "the Carpets"), which is Latinized as *Stromata*. In English it is known as *The Miscellanies*. Abbreviated *Strom.* or *Misc.*

Epiphanius of Salamis. The Greek title of his major work is *Panarion* (literally, "the Medicine Chest"). Its Latin title is *Adversus Haereses* ("Against Heresies"), and it's usually cited as *Haereses*. Usually abbreviated *Haer.* or *Adv. haer.*, but sometimes *Pan.* (Compare with Irenaeus and Hippolytus.)

Eusebius Pamphili, Bishop of Caesarea (not to be confused with Pamphilus of Caesarea, who was the bishop there before him). His major work is written in Greek but is usually known by its Latin title, *Historia Ecclesiastica* ("Church History"). Abbreviated *Hist. eccl.* or *H.E.*

Hippolytus of Rome. All his works were originally written in Greek. His first anti-heresy writing is entitled *Syntagma* (literally, "Arrangement"). The work itself is lost, but parts of it survive in quotations. Its Latin title is *Adversum omnes Haereses* ("Against All Heresies"). Note that the Latin word for *against* has two forms, *adversus* and *adversum*, with no difference in meaning, just as English has *toward* and *towards*, and *among* and *amongst*. Often abbreviated *Adv. omn. haer.*

His second anti-heresy writing is entitled in Greek *Philosophouma* (or *Kata Pason Haireseon Elenchos*). It is called the *Refutatio Omnium Haeresium* in Latin, and the *Refutation of All Heresies* in English. Abbreviated *Ref. omn. haer.* (Compare with Epiphanius and Irenaeus.)

Irenaeus of Lyons. His major work is written in Greek but is usually known by its Latin title, *Adversus Haereses* ("Against Heresies"). Abbreviated *Haer.* or *Adv. haer.* (Compare with Epiphanius and Hippolytus.)

Jerome (his name in Latin is Eusebius Hieronymus). His "Commentary on Matthew" is written in Latin and its Latin title is *Commentarium in Matthaeum*. Note that the Latin word for *commentary* may be either masculine or neuter: *commentarius* or *commentarium*. Abbreviated with his name as Hier. *Comm. in Matt.* (Compare with Origen.)

Another of Jerome's writings, *Adversus Pelagianos Dialogi* (or *Dialogi contra Pelagianos*), is known in English as "The Dialogue against the Pelagians." Abbreviated *Adv. Pelag.*

Origen. His "Commentary on Matthew" is written in Greek but is usually known by its Latin title, *Commentarium in Matthaeum*. It survives only in Jerome's Latin translation and is therefore often included among Jerome's works, but is not to be confused with Jerome's own commentary on Matthew. Abbreviated with his name as Orig. *Comm. in Matt.* (Compare with Jerome.)

Philaster of Brescia. His major work, written in Latin, is entitled *Diversarum Haereseon Liber* ("The Book of Assorted Heresies"). It has a Greek word in its title, *haereseon*, in the genitive plural. The work is also called *Liber de Haeresibus* ("The Book about Heresies"). Abbreviated *Div. haer. lib.* or *Lib. de haer.*

List of Selected References

Evans, Craig A. *Noncanonical Writings and New Testament Interpretation* (1992).

Klijn, A.F.J., and G.J. Reinink. *Patristic Evidence for Jewish-Christian Sects* (Leiden, 1973).

Migne, J.-P. (editor). *Patrologia Graeca* series and *Patrologia Latina* series (Paris, 1844-1858).

Pritz, Ray A. *Nazarene Jewish Christianity* (Jerusalem, 1992).

von Dobschütz, Ernst. *Das Decretum Gelasianum de libris recipiendis et non recipiendis.* Reproduced in *Texte und Untersuchungen*, vol. 38 (Leipzig, 1912).

Zahn, Theodor, *Geschichte des Neutestamentlichen Kanons* (Erlangen & Leipzig, 1890).

All Scripture quotations
are from the King James Bible.